# Contents

Introduction  *page xi*
How to use this book  *xii*

## Part I  Kinds of words  *1*

### Unit 1  Nouns  *3*

Lesson 1  Identifying nouns  *3*
Lesson 2  Concrete and abstract nouns  *5*
Lesson 3  Singular and plural nouns  *9*
Lesson 4  Animate and inanimate nouns  *12*
Lesson 5  Count and noncount nouns  *14*
Lesson 6  Proper and common nouns  *18*
Answer keys: *Test yourself* questions – Unit 1  *20*

### Unit 2  Verbs  *23*

Lesson 7  Identifying verbs  *23*
Lesson 8  The verb base  *25*
Lesson 9  Action verbs and linking verbs  *27*
Lesson 10  Transitive and intransitive verbs  *35*
Lesson 11  Phrasal verbs  *38*
Answer keys: *Test yourself* questions – Unit 2  *41*

### Unit 3  Determiners  *45*

Lesson 12  Articles  *46*
Lesson 13  Demonstratives  *48*
Lesson 14  Possessives  *50*
Lesson 15  Quantifiers  *53*
Answer keys: *Test yourself* questions – Unit 3  *55*

### Unit 4  Adjectives  *58*

Lesson 16  Identifying adjectives  *58*
Answer keys: *Test yourself* questions – Unit 4  *63*

### Unit 5  Prepositions  *65*

Lesson 17  Identifying prepositions  *65*
Answer keys: *Test yourself* questions – Unit 5  *68*

### Unit 6  Conjunctions  *69*

Lesson 18  Coordinating conjunctions  *70*
Lesson 19  Subordinating conjunctions  *73*

## Contents

  Lesson 20 Correlative conjunctions *77*
  Answer keys: *Test yourself* questions – Unit 6 *79*

### Unit 7 Pronouns *81*

  Lesson 21 Subject and object pronouns *82*
  Lesson 22 Reflexive pronouns *85*
  Lesson 23 Demonstrative pronouns *87*
  Lesson 24 Possessive pronouns *89*
  Lesson 25 Interrogative pronouns *93*
  Lesson 26 Relative pronouns *96*
  Answer keys: *Test yourself* questions – Unit 7 *99*

### Unit 8 Adverbs *103*

  Lesson 27 Identifying adverbs *103*
  Answer keys: *Test yourself* questions – Unit 8 *107*

Review matching exercise and answer key – Part I *109*

## Part II Kinds of phrases *111*

### Unit 9 Noun phrases *113*

  Lesson 28 The basic structure of noun phrases *113*
  Answer keys: *Test yourself* questions – Unit 9 *119*

### Unit 10 Prepositional phrases *121*

  Lesson 29 The basic structure of prepositional phrases *121*
  Answer keys: *Test yourself* questions – Unit 10 *125*

### Unit 11 Verb phrases *126*

  Lesson 30 The basic structure of verb phrases *126*
  Answer keys: *Test yourself* questions – Unit 11 *135*

### Unit 12 Auxiliary phrases *138*

  Lesson 31 The basic structure of auxiliary phrases *139*
  Lesson 32 Modals *141*
  Lesson 33 Perfect *have* *143*
  Lesson 34 Progressive *be* *146*
  Lesson 35 Combining auxiliary verbs *148*
  Lesson 36 The suffixes of auxiliary verbs *151*
  Lesson 37 Tense *156*
  Answer keys: *Test yourself* questions – Unit 12 *164*

### Unit 13 Subjects and objects *169*

  Lesson 38 Subjects *170*
  Lesson 39 Direct objects *173*
  Lesson 40 Indirect objects *177*
  Lesson 41 The functions of pronouns *183*

       Lesson 42  Implied subjects: commands   *186*
       Answer keys: *Test yourself* questions – Unit 13   *189*

## Unit 14  Compound phrases   *193*

       Lesson 43  Compound noun phrases   *194*
       Lesson 44  Compound verb phrases   *195*
       Answer keys: *Test yourself* questions – Unit 14   *197*

Review matching exercise and answer key – Part II   *198*

# Introduction

Our goal in this book is to help you learn about English grammar in as simple and straightforward a way as possible. The book was inspired by our students, most of whom panic when we say words like *adjective*, *subject*, and *passive*. We believe that panic will be replaced by knowledge and confidence as readers work their way through this user-friendly book.

Who is this book for? It's for anyone who needs or wants to understand English grammar. That includes readers who: (1) want to improve their writing; (2) are studying a foreign language; (3) are or want to be teachers; (4) are learning English as a second language; (5) are or want to be professionals such as speech-language pathologists and attorneys; (6) are interested in how English works. The book is self-guided and self-paced; it can be used alone or as part of a course.

The workbook approach used here will move you beyond simply labeling words to an understanding of how the different pieces of a sentence fit together. To help you achieve this understanding, we present information in small steps, with many opportunities to apply each new piece of information in exercises before you move on to the next step.

Like all languages, English is a collection of dialects. While society views some of these dialects as having more social prestige than others, when we look at them objectively we find that all dialects are equal linguistically. That means that all dialects have grammatical rules, and the grammatical rules of one dialect are no more precise, pure, or logical than the grammatical rules of another dialect. Nonetheless, in this book we focus on the grammar of Standard American English because it is widely known and because writing requires a knowledge of formal, standard English.

We deliberately limit this introductory book in both content and complexity. Wherever possible, we provide you with a simple rule of thumb to use. However, we don't claim to cover all of English sentence structure. A clear understanding of what usually works will give you a foundation for recognizing and understanding the exceptions. Our aim is to provide you with the basics.

This book will clarify English sentence structure and provide you with a useful reference book that you can turn to long after you've completed the exercises. It will also provide you with a solid foundation for more advanced study.

So take a deep breath and turn the page. We predict that it won't hurt a bit. In fact, you may be surprised to find out how easy *English Grammar* can be.

## How to use this book

**What are the features of this book that will help you use it effectively?**
- We assume no prior knowledge of English grammar. Depending on your background and interest, you can either work the book through from cover to cover or just read about selected topics.
- We utilize user-friendly, easy-to-understand language, avoiding excessive technical terminology.
- Information is presented in lesson format; most lessons are short, helping to make the material manageable.
- Numerous exercises allow you to test yourself after new information is presented; the exercises gradually incorporate more knowledge while building on prior information.
- Each exercise has a sample item done for you, to help you with the exercise.
- Each exercise is separated into two parts: *Getting started* and *More practice*. With each *Getting started* part, we provide a page reference to the answers, so you'll immediately know whether or not you're on the right track. For *More practice* items, answers are provided on the accompanying website.
- In addition to exercises, each lesson contains easy to find *Quick tips*. These provide convenient "tricks" to help you master the material or highlight the main concepts in each lesson.
- We've also included short sections called *To enhance your understanding*. These sections are intended for those of you who are interested in more than basic information. These sections can easily be skipped by beginners; they're not necessary for understanding any material later on in the book.
- Throughout the text, ungrammatical sentences are identified with an asterisk (*) at the beginning.

**How is this book organized?**
- The book has three parts: Part I deals with types of words, Part II with types of phrases, and Part III with types of sentences.
- Each part is divided into units and each unit is subdivided into related lessons.
- Each lesson contains ample *Test yourself* exercises. Each exercise has ten questions, with answer keys provided at the end of each unit and on the accompanying website.
- A review matching exercise with an answer key is included at the end of each part.
- Additional review exercises for each unit are provided on the companion website.
- For easy reference, the end of the book contains a list of all *Quick tips*, a detailed glossary, and an index.

# PART I: KINDS OF WORDS

Do you shudder when you hear the words *noun* or *verb*? Don't worry – you already know all about word categories, also known as parts of speech, though you may not think you do. You know, for example, that you can say *the idea* and *the boy* but not *\*the about* or *\*happy the*. (As stated in the *How to use this book* section, an asterisk [*] is used to indicate that something is ungrammatical.) That is, you know that some words can go in some places in a sentence and others can't. A word category, or part of speech, is just a name given to a group of words that have something in common, such as where they can go in a sentence. Part I gives you a quick and easy guide to basic word categories.

## UNIT 1: NOUNS

# Lesson 1: Identifying nouns

Nouns are commonly defined as words that refer to a person, place, thing, or idea. How can you identify a noun?

> **Quick tip 1.1**
>
> If you can put the word *the* in front of a word and it sounds like a unit, the word is a noun.

For example, *the boy* sounds like a unit, so *boy* is a noun. *The chair* sounds like a unit, so *chair* is a noun. Compare these nouns to *\*the very*, *\*the walked*, *\*the because*. *Very*, *walked*, and *because* are not nouns. While you can easily put *the* and *very* together (for example, *the very tall boy*), *the very*, by itself, does not work as a unit while *the chair* does. So, *chair* is a noun; *very* is not. (There is one kind of noun that cannot always have *the* in front of it; see Lesson 6 later in this unit.)

### Test yourself 1.1

Which of the following words are nouns? See if they sound like a unit when you put them here: *the* _____. Check the appropriate column.

|  | Noun | Not a noun |
|---|---|---|
| Sample: always |  | x |

*Getting started* (answers on p. 20)

1. tree
2. when
3. beds
4. glass
5. said

*More practice* (answers on the website)

6. slowly
7. factory
8. ticket
9. boxes
10. almost

### Test yourself 1.2

Underline the nouns in these phrases. Test each word to see if it sounds like a unit when you put it here: *the* _____.
Sample: all my <u>friends</u>

*Getting started* (answers on p. 20)

1. your red sweater
2. those boxes
3. a few men
4. many digital photos
5. his very interesting article

## UNIT 1: NOUNS

***More practice*** (answers on the website)

6. their carpets
7. a hand-painted plate
8. the court stenographer
9. our psychology professor
10. two interesting museums

# Lesson 2: Concrete and abstract nouns

Here's an unusual sentence: *He smelled the marriage.* What makes this sentence unusual is that we don't generally think of the noun *marriage* as something that can be smelled. Some nouns are **concrete**: they can be perceived by our senses – they are things that we can see, hear, smell, taste, or touch. Those nouns that are not concrete are **abstract**. *Marriage* is something abstract, so it's odd to say it's being perceived by one of our senses, our sense of smell.

The nouns in Lesson 1 were all concrete nouns. Other nouns, such as *marriage*, are abstract; this means that they refer to things that you cannot perceive with your senses, things you cannot see, smell, feel, taste, or touch. Here are some more concrete and abstract nouns:

| Concrete | Abstract |
|---|---|
| newspaper | love |
| heel | honesty |
| glass | culture |
| jewelry | mind |

> **Quick tip 2.1**
>
> Concrete nouns refer to things we can perceive with one of our senses. Abstract nouns cannot be perceived by our senses.

## Test yourself 2.1

Decide if each noun is concrete or abstract.
Sample: discussion   abstract

*Getting started* (answers on p. 20)

1. muffin
2. violin
3. freedom
4. elegance
5. train

*More practice* (answers on the website)

6. friend
7. friendliness
8. economics
9. dormitory
10. capitalism

## Test yourself 2.2

Which of the following words are nouns? See if they sound like a unit when you put them here: the _____. The nouns will all be abstract nouns. Check the appropriate column.

|  | Noun | Not a noun |
|---|---|---|
| Sample: confusion | ✗ | |

# UNIT 1: NOUNS

*Getting started* (answers on p. 20)

1. concept
2. shockingly
3. wrote
4. conversation
5. interview

*More practice* (answers on the website)

6. ran
7. secret
8. her
9. death
10. job

An abstract noun is sometimes easier to identify if you create a sentence with it. For example, *the happiness* is a unit, as can be seen in *The happiness on her face delighted him*. Thus, *happiness* is a noun. Here are some other abstract nouns in sentences; the nouns are underlined.

1. It was not the complaint which bothered him.
2. They were attempting to stop the abuse.
3. The joy which they felt was obvious.

Another easy way to identify a noun, especially an abstract noun, is to put the word *his* (or other words like it – see Lesson 21) in front of it and see if it sounds like a unit. For example, *his complaint, his happiness, his concern* all are units; therefore, *complaint, happiness*, and *concern* are nouns.

> **Quick tip 2.2**
>
> If you can put *his* in front of a word and it sounds like a unit, the word is a noun.

## Test yourself 2.3

Which of the following words are nouns? See if they sound like a unit when you put them here: *his* _____. The nouns will all be abstract nouns. Check the appropriate column.

|  | Noun | Not a noun |
|---|---|---|
| Sample: obligation | x | |

*Getting started* (answers on p. 20)

1. jumped
2. appropriate
3. popularity
4. emotions
5. real

*More practice* (answers on the website)

6. closed
7. celebration
8. their
9. news
10. spoken

## Test yourself 2.4

Which of the following words are nouns? These are a mix of concrete and abstract nouns. Check the appropriate column.

|  | Noun | Not a noun |
|---|---|---|
| Sample: while | | x |

*Lesson 2: Concrete and abstract nouns*

***Getting started*** (answers on p. 21)

1. repair
2. intelligence
3. a
4. skis
5. us

***More practice*** (answers on the website)

6. obstruction
7. pounds
8. disgraceful
9. complicated
10. since

## Test yourself 2.5

Underline the nouns in the sentences below. In this exercise, the nouns will all have *the* or *his* in front of them. Some will be concrete and some will be abstract. Some sentences have more than one noun.
Sample: His answer wasn't helpful.

***Getting started*** (answers on p. 21)

1. She read the play over again.
2. The actions became monotonous.
3. He felt that his marriage, his relationship with her, was strong.
4. The time had finally come to confess the truth.
5. He's the boy who delivers the paper.

***More practice*** (answers on the website)

6. The glitterati always like to follow the fashion of the day.
7. They will repair his stove.
8. The arrangement was good for all of them.
9. The audience stared at the screen, fascinated by the action they were seeing.
10. The definition was in his dictionary.

The nouns are underlined in the following sentences:
    4. This author lives with her husband.
    5. Do most people proceed contentedly through life?
    6. Your photograph of that child sleeping won you a prize.
As you can see from these sentences, while *the* _____ or *his* _____ are ways to test a word to see if it's a noun, a noun doesn't necessarily have *the* or *his* in front of it in every sentence. Since we can say *the author, the husband, the people, his life, the photograph, his child,* and *his prize,* the underlined words in sentences 4–6 are each nouns.

## Test yourself 2.6

Underline the nouns in the sentences below. In this exercise, the nouns will not all have *the* or *his* in front of them. Just test each word to see if it can be a noun.
Sample: The repair of my camera went smoothly.

***Getting started*** (answers on p. 21)

1. I wrote every word of the letter.
2. The house was near the city.
3. Why did he get on an elevator?
4. She has my phone.
5. Your younger brother was busy.

***More practice*** (answers on the website)

6. A group of three generals sent the troops away.
7. The flag was near your desk.
8. My mother acted in a play.
9. He called the house every day.
10. You have to give her salary and benefits.

# UNIT 1: NOUNS

It's important to realize that the same word can often be used as more than one part of speech. For example, *repair* can be used as a noun (example: *The repair was relatively inexpensive*), as an adjective (example: *The repair manual was not very helpful*), or as a verb (example: *He needs to repair the washing machine*). We'll talk about verbs and adjectives in Units 2 and 4, respectively.

# Lesson 3: Singular and plural nouns

What's the difference between *cat* and *cats*? The noun *cat* is used when it refers to only one cat; its form is **singular**. The noun *cats* is used when it represents more than one cat; its form is **plural**. Thus, the singular and plural forms tell us about **number**. Below are some nouns in their singular and plural forms.

| Singular | Plural |
|---|---|
| box | boxes |
| bed | beds |
| kite | kites |
| day | days |
| country | countries |
| man | men |
| child | children |

## Test yourself 3.1

Underline each noun in the sentences below and indicate whether it is singular (SG) or plural (PL). There may be more than one noun in a sentence.
Sample: They used her <u>computer</u> (SG) to download the <u>files</u> (PL).

*Getting started* (answers on p. 21)

1. He had a few good ideas.
2. The boys spoke in a quiet whisper.
3. The tourists greeted the queen with attitudes of respect.
4. My neighbor is a neurologist.
5. The exterminator found bugs in the office.

*More practice* (answers on the website)

6. Sharks live in water.
7. Yesterday, I caught a big trout.
8. There are many beautiful homes on this block.
9. Visitors to this country must obtain visas.
10. His cousin fought in a brutal battle to free ninety hostages.

### Regular and irregular plurals

Usually, we pluralize a noun by adding an "s" to it, as in *books*; these nouns are called **regular**. There are a handful of nouns that are pluralized in other ways; these nouns are called **irregular**.

Irregular nouns form their plural in different ways. Here are some common patterns:
1. changing a vowel: *man/men*, for example
2. adding "ren" or "en": *child/children*, for example
3. adding nothing: *fish/fish*, for example
4. changing "f" to "v" and then adding "s": *knife/knives*, for example

## Test yourself 3.2

Underline each plural noun in the sentences below and indicate if it is regular (REG) or irregular (IRREG) in terms of how it is pluralized.
Sample: The <u>women</u> (IRREG) received their education at some exclusive <u>schools</u> (REG).

## UNIT 1: NOUNS

***Getting started*** (answers on p. 21)

1. The doctor treated most of the patients who were waiting.
2. The geese crossed the road near my car.
3. She set a trap to catch the mice that had invaded her kitchen.
4. You will have to feed the oxen most afternoons.
5. Whenever I travel to the countryside, I see many sheep, ducks, deer, and cows.

***More practice*** (answers on the website)

6. Those husbands and wives lead interesting lives.
7. Her feet have grown since last year.
8. The back window of my apartment overlooks about a dozen roofs.
9. The salesmen surrounded me in the showroom.
10. Kenneth had to buy two bottles of disinfectant to get rid of the lice in his bathroom.

### To enhance your understanding

What is the plural of the "word" *blun*? Even though you've probably never seen this nonsense word, you're likely to say its plural is *bluns*. That's because we don't have to memorize the ending of regular plurals; we simply use our plural formation rule: "add *s*." But the forms for irregular plural words, like *children* and *men*, need to be memorized since they don't follow a consistent pattern.

### To further enhance your understanding

Earlier we said that we usually pluralize a noun in English by adding an "s" to it. There's actually more to it than that, when one examines the pronunciation of regular nouns more closely.

Here are some regular English nouns:

| A | B |
|---|---|
| cat | dog |
| lip | bee |
| myth | car |
| laugh | deal |

Say each word in column A out loud, adding its plural ending. (Don't whisper, or this won't work.) You'll notice that, as you expect, you're adding an [s] sound to each word. (Symbols in square brackets [ ] indicate sounds rather than letters.) Now say each word in column B out loud, adding its plural ending. If you listen carefully, you'll notice that you're not adding an [s] sound to each word to make it plural. You're actually adding a [z] sound! (If English is not your native language, you may not be doing this.)

It turns out that we learned, when we were acquiring English as children, that it is the last *sound*, and not *letter*, of a regular noun that determines whether we add [s] or [z]. Some sounds (voiced sounds) are made with our vocal cords vibrating, like the strings of a guitar. Try this: hold your hand touching your throat, about where a man's Adam's apple is, while you say and hold a [v] sound ([v v v v v . . .]). You'll feel the vibration of your vocal cords.

Other sounds (voiceless sounds) are made with our vocal cords not vibrating. Now touch your hand to your throat again and this time say and hold an [f] sound ([f f f f f . . . ]); you will notice the lack of vibration.

So how do we know whether to say the plural with an [s] or [z] sound? If the last sound of a word is a voiceless sound, we add an [s] sound to make it plural. If the last sound of a word is a voiced sound, we add a [z] sound to make it plural. This is not a rule that someone has ever taught us, but part of our unconscious knowledge of English.

Notice that having an [s] sound after voiceless sounds makes sense: [s] itself is voiceless. By the same reasoning, having a [z] after voiced sounds also makes sense: [z] itself is voiced. So what you can see is that the last sound of the noun and the sound of the regular plural share the same voicing characteristic: either the vocal cords vibrate for both sounds, or they don't.

You may have noticed that there's actually a third type of regular noun. Say the following words out loud, adding the plural ending to each:

| glass | garage |
|-------|--------|
| maze  | church |
| wish  | judge  |

These words all already end in sounds (again, not letters) that are either [s] or [z] or sounds very similar to them. They are all "noisy" sounds. For the plural forms of these words, we add a vowel sound (written with the letter e) followed by a [z] sound (but written with the letter s): glasses, mazes, wishes, garages, churches, judges. If you think about it, pronouncing a vowel between the noisy sound at the end of the noun and the noisy sound [z] of the plural makes sense: without that vowel, we would have two noisy sounds in a row, something that would be harder for the listener to hear clearly.

Wow! You may want to just pause for a moment here and contemplate the complexity of what you know about your language. And you knew how to do this before you even went to kindergarten! You just haven't known that you know it.

# Lesson 4: Animate and inanimate nouns

Take a look at the following sentence:
1. *The postcard saw the mailman.*

What's strange about this sentence? What's strange is that we don't expect a postcard, which is not alive, to be able to see something; only things that are alive have the ability to see. Nouns that refer to things that are alive are called **animate**, while nouns that refer to things that are not alive are called **inanimate**. *Postcard* is an inanimate noun and using it as an animate one makes for a very unusual sentence.

> **Quick tip 4.1**
>
> Animate nouns refer to things that are alive; inanimate nouns refer to things that are not alive.

## Test yourself 4.1

Decide if each noun is animate or inanimate.
Sample: apple   inanimate

*Getting started* (answers on p. 21)

1. word
2. lizard
3. glasses
4. calendar
5. baby

*More practice* (answers on the website)

6. criminal
7. furniture
8. doctor
9. mouse
10. truck

Now take a look at the following sentence:
2. *The dog wrote a best-selling novel.*

Again, there's something strange here. We know that *dog* is animate. However, only a special type of animate noun has the ability to write a best-selling novel: a **human** noun. The following sentence is fine, since *teacher* is a human animate noun: *My teacher wrote a best-selling novel.* On the other hand, since *dog* is a **nonhuman** animate noun, sentence 2 does not sound right.

To summarize: nouns may be human animate *(teacher)*, nonhuman animate *(dog)*, or inanimate *(postcard)*.

## Test yourself 4.2

Decide if each noun is animate or inanimate. If a noun is animate, decide if it is human or nonhuman.
Sample: chair   inanimate

*Lesson 4: Animate and inanimate nouns*

***Getting started*** (answers on p. 21)

1. dinner
2. pet
3. friend
4. child
5. spider

***More practice*** (answers on the website)

6. tablecloth
7. recipes
8. assassin
9. shark
10. freedom

# Lesson 5: Count and noncount nouns

Let's take a closer look at the noun *hand*. Notice that you can say the following:

    the hand    a hand    hands

Here are some other nouns which demonstrate the same pattern:

    the store    a store    stores
    the idea    an idea    ideas
    the tissue    a tissue    tissues

Let's compare *hand* to the noun *furniture*. As with *hand*, we can say *the furniture*. But we can't say *\*a furniture* or *\*furnitures*. Here are some other nouns which demonstrate the same pattern as *furniture*:

    the dust    *a dust    *dusts
    the energy    *an energy    *energies
    the biology    *a biology    *biologies

Thus, there are some nouns that can be counted, and so we can use *a* or *an* with them and can also make them plural. These nouns are called, appropriately, **count** nouns. *Hand* is a count noun. So are *store*, *idea*, and *tissue*.

There are other nouns that typically are not counted, and so we do not use *a* or *an* with them and do not typically make them plural. These nouns are called, also appropriately, **noncount** nouns. (Another name for a noncount noun is a **mass** noun.) *Furniture* is a noncount noun. So are *dust*, *energy*, and *biology*.

You may well be saying to yourself, "Wait a minute. I can count furniture. I can say something like: three couches and three chairs make six pieces of furniture." And of course, you'd be right. But notice that in this sentence, the words *couch* and *chair* can be made plural, but not the word *furniture*. And the word *piece* can be made plural, but, again, not the word *furniture*.

> **Quick tip 5.1**
>
> If you can pluralize a noun in a sentence, it is functioning as a count noun.

Note that a noun is considered to be a count noun if it can be made plural, even if it's not plural in a particular sentence. Thus, in the sentence *I ate a cookie*, *cookie* is a count noun because one could pluralize it to *cookies* without changing its basic meaning.

## Test yourself 5.1

For each underlined noun in the sentences below, indicate if it is count (C) or noncount (NC). Use the plural test to help you.

*Lesson 5: Count and noncount nouns*

Sample: Her hairstyle (C) clearly revealed her face.

*Getting started* (answers on p. 22)
1. The lights (    ) of the city (    ) twinkled.
2. I love eating rice (    ).
3. His anger (    ) was barely under control.
4. Her job (    ) was rather demanding.
5. Many types of information (    ) are available at the library (    ).

*More practice* (answers on the website)
6. The police (    ) will be here in a moment.
7. He leaned on the handle (    ) and cursed.
8. I was so thirsty, I needed three glasses (    ) of water (    ).
9. How much money (    ) do you make in an hour (    )?
10. By 11 P.M., the train-station (    ) was nearly empty.

There is also another good way to decide if a noun is count or noncount. Take a look at the use of the words *much* and *many* in the following sentences.
1. He has many children.
2. That man has many interests.
3. That will take too much time.
4. They have many lights on in the house.
5. We have much furniture in our store.
6. I wonder how much wealth is in Silicon Valley.

As you may have noticed, *many* is used with count nouns, *much* is used with noncount nouns.

> **Quick tip 5.2**
>
> If you can use *many* with a noun (when it is pluralized), it's a count noun. If you can use *much* with a noun, it's a noncount noun.

And we have still another way to distinguish count from noncount nouns:
7. He has fewer children than I do.
8. That man has fewer interests than he used to.
9. That will take less time than I thought.
10. They have fewer lights on in the house.
11. We have less furniture in our store.
12. I don't have less money in my purse than you have.

As you've probably figured out from these examples, we use *fewer* with count nouns and *less* with noncount nouns.

> **Quick tip 5.3**
>
> If you can use *fewer* with a noun (when it is pluralized), it's a count noun. If you can use *less* with a noun, it's a noncount noun.

15

# UNIT 1: NOUNS

## Test yourself 5.2

For each underlined noun in the sentences below, indicate if it is being used as a count (C) or noncount (NC) noun in that sentence. Use the plural, *much/many*, or *fewer/less* tests to help you.
Sample: Their new album (C) was a huge hit.

*Getting started* (answers on p. 22)

1. Algebra ( ) was one of my worst subjects ( ) in high school ( ).
2. I had no idea that there were various theories ( ), such as Euclidean and fractal.
3. The smoke ( ) rose through the chimney ( ).
4. Bread ( ) is a staple in many societies ( ).
5. She decided to push the issue ( ) further.

*More practice* (answers on the website)

6. People ( ) are funny sometimes.
7. The government ( ) of the United States has three branches ( ).
8. Senators ( ) can spend money ( ) unnecessarily.
9. It takes effort ( ) to get a good grade ( ) in Mr. Goodman's class ( ).
10. The reporters ( ) wrote the story ( ).

### To enhance your understanding

Many nouns can be used as either count nouns or as noncount nouns, depending on how they are being used in a specific sentence. Let's look at the following sentence containing the word *sugar*:

    13. The sugar is spilling onto the floor.

In this sentence, is *sugar* being used as a count or noncount noun? Would you say: *The sugars are spilling onto the floor*? or *Many sugars are spilling onto the floor*? Probably not. So *sugar*, in sentence 13, is a noncount noun.

    Now take a look at another sentence with *sugar*:

    14. This gourmet shop has sugars I've never even heard of.

In this sentence, is *sugar* being used as a count or noncount noun? First, notice that *sugar* here is pluralized. Second, notice that you can say *This gourmet shop has many sugars I've never even heard of*. So *sugar*, in sentence 14, is a count noun. In terms of meaning, what is important here is that the sentence is talking about different types of sugars, say, brown sugar, white sugar, confectioners' sugar, etc.

    And one more sentence type with *sugar*:

    15. The sugar that works best in this recipe is brown sugar.

Here, *sugar*, while not pluralized, could be pluralized and refers, in fact, to a kind of sugar. For example, you could say: *The sugars that work best in this recipe are brown sugar and white sugar*. For these reasons, *sugar* is being used here as a count noun.

    Here are some more examples of sentences with nouns which, like *sugar*, are typically used as noncount nouns but can also be used as count nouns.

        16a. I like to drink milk. (*milk* used as noncount noun)
        16b. That store has milks with different kinds of flavoring: chocolate, vanilla, mocha, and strawberry. (*milks* used as count noun)

*Lesson 5: Count and noncount nouns*

> 16c. The milk that is the healthiest is nonfat milk. (*milk* used as count noun)
> 17a. A plentiful supply of water is important for a community's survival. (*water* used as noncount noun)
> 17b. There are different kinds of gourmet waters on the market these days. (*waters* used as count noun)
> 17c. The water I usually order in restaurants is imported. (*water* used as count noun)

# Lesson 6: Proper and common nouns

Do the following sentences look a little strange?
1. Mrs. smith took the 10th grade class of lincoln high school to france for a trip.
2. The class visited paris and was thrilled to see the eiffel tower.

Normally, we capitalize the first letter of nouns that are actual names, no matter where they are in a sentence. Let's look at the same sentences with the names capitalized:
3. Mrs. Smith took the 10th grade class of Lincoln High School to France for a trip.
4. The class visited Paris and was thrilled to see the Eiffel Tower.

Nouns that are actual names are called **proper** nouns; nouns that are not names are called **common** nouns. Notice that not only people have names: places (*Rome*), companies (*IBM*), and books (*Gone With the Wind*), among others, can have names, too.

> **Quick tip 6.1**
>
> Nouns that are actual names, for example *Mary*, are called proper nouns. Nouns that are not names are called common nouns, e.g. *girl*.

> **Quick tip 6.2**
>
> One way to identify a proper noun is to ask yourself: is this a noun I would capitalize, no matter where it is in a sentence? If so, it's a proper noun.

## Test yourself 6.1

For each noun below, determine if it is a proper noun or common noun. For this exercise, the proper nouns are not capitalized.
Sample: england   proper

**Getting started** (answers on p. 22)

1. seattle
2. crater lake national park
3. tissues
4. sofa
5. pepsi cola

**More practice** (answers on the website)

6. mediterranean sea
7. disneyland
8. company
9. british broadcasting company
10. television

*Lesson 6: Proper and common nouns*

**To enhance your understanding**

In Lesson 1 we said that words that can have *the* in front of them and sound like a complete unit are nouns. That still works. The reverse, however, is not true: not all proper nouns can have *the* in front of them. Compare the following proper nouns. Those on the left use *the*; those on the right do not.

5.  a. The United States      Great Britain
        The Netherlands      France
    b. The Holy See      Holy Cross University
    c. The Jolly Green Giant      Big Foot
    d. The Bronx      Manhattan

Most proper nouns don't use *the* – just think of the names of people you know. Those few cases where a proper noun does use *the* are exceptions; we memorize those.

# Answer keys: *Test yourself, Getting started questions – Unit 1*

## Test yourself 1.1

|   | Noun | Not a noun |
|---|---|---|
| 1. tree | x |  |
| 2. when |  | x |
| 3. beds | x |  |
| 4. glass | x |  |
| 5. said |  | x |

## Test yourself 1.2

1. your red <u>sweater</u>
2. those <u>boxes</u>
3. a few <u>men</u>
4. many digital <u>photos</u>
5. his very interesting <u>article</u>

## Test yourself 2.1

| 1. muffin | concrete |
|---|---|
| 2. violin | concrete |
| 3. freedom | abstract |
| 4. elegance | abstract |
| 5. train | concrete |

## Test yourself 2.2

|   | Noun | Not a noun |
|---|---|---|
| 1. concept | x |  |
| 2. shockingly |  | x |
| 3. wrote |  | x |
| 4. conversation | x |  |
| 5. interview | x |  |

## Test yourself 2.3

|   | Noun | Not a noun |
|---|---|---|
| 1. jumped |  | x |
| 2. appropriate |  | x |
| 3. popularity | x |  |
| 4. emotions | x |  |
| 5. real |  | x |

Answer keys: Unit 1

## Test yourself 2.4

|   | Noun | Not a noun |
|---|---|---|
| 1. repair | x |  |
| 2. intelligence | x |  |
| 3. a |  | x |
| 4. skis | x |  |
| 5. us |  | x |

## Test yourself 2.5

1. She read the play over again.
2. The actions became monotonous.
3. He felt that his marriage, his relationship with her, was strong.
4. The time had finally come to confess the truth.
5. He's the boy who delivers the paper.

## Test yourself 2.6

1. I wrote every word of the letter.
2. The house was near the city.
3. Why did he get on an elevator?
4. She has my phone.
5. Your younger brother was busy.

## Test yourself 3.1

1. He had a few good ideas (PL).
2. The boys (PL) spoke in a quiet whisper (SG).
3. The tourists (PL) greeted the queen (SG) with attitudes (PL) of respect (SG).
4. My neighbor (SG) is a neurologist (SG).
5. The exterminator (SG) found bugs (PL) in the office (SG).

## Test yourself 3.2

1. The doctor treated most of the patients (REG) who were waiting.
2. The geese (IRREG) crossed the road near my car.
3. She set a trap to catch the mice (IRREG) that had invaded her kitchen.
4. You will have to feed the oxen (IRREG) most afternoons (REG).
5. Whenever I travel to the countryside, I see many sheep (IRREG), ducks (REG), deer (IRREG), and cows (REG).

## Test yourself 4.1

| 1. word | inanimate |
| 2. lizard | animate |
| 3. glasses | inanimate |
| 4. calendar | inanimate |
| 5. baby | animate |

## Test yourself 4.2

| 1. dinner | inanimate |
| 2. pet | nonhuman animate |

21

# UNIT 1: NOUNS

3. friend      human animate
4. child       human animate
5. spider      nonhuman animate

## Test yourself 5.1

1. The lights (C) of the city (C) twinkled.
2. I love eating rice (NC).
3. His anger (NC) was barely under control.
4. Her job (C) was rather demanding.
5. Many types of information (NC) are available at the library (C).

## Test yourself 5.2

1. Algebra (NC) was one of my worst subjects (C) in high school (C).
2. I had no idea that there were various theories (C), such as Euclidean and fractal.
3. The smoke (NC) rose through the chimney (C).
4. Bread (NC) is a staple in many societies (C).
5. She decided to push the issue (C) further.

## Test yourself 6.1

1. seattle                      proper
2. crater lake national park    proper
3. tissues                      common
4. sofa                         common
5. pepsi cola                   proper

☞ **FOR A REVIEW EXERCISE OF THIS UNIT, SEE THE WEBSITE.**

## UNIT 2: VERBS

# Lesson 7: Identifying verbs

What's a verb? **Verbs** are words that usually express an action. Here are two easy ways to identify a verb; you can use either one.

> **Quick tip 7.1**
>
> If a word can have *should* in front of it and the phrase sounds complete, the word is a verb. Examples: *should leave, should sail, should discover, should complain*. *Leave, sail, discover,* and *complain* are all verbs.

> **Quick tip 7.2**
>
> If a word can have *to* in front of it and the phrase sounds complete, it's a verb. Examples: *to leave, to sail, to discover, to complain. Leave, sail, discover,* and *complain* are all verbs. (Note that we're not talking here about *two, too,* or the *to* that indicates direction, as in *Let's go to the park.*)

Here are some examples of verbs. You can see that they all meet the test with *should* and the test with *to*.

| go: | should go | to go |
| --- | --- | --- |
| tell: | should tell | to tell |
| disagree: | should disagree | to disagree |
| spell: | should spell | to spell |

In contrast, the following words do not pass the *should* or *to* test:

| coffee: | *should coffee | *to coffee |
| --- | --- | --- |
| beautiful: | *should beautiful | *to beautiful |
| hardly: | *should hardly | *to hardly |
| under: | *should under | *to under |

Thus, *coffee, beautiful, hardly,* and *under* are not verbs.

## Test yourself 7.1

Which of the following words are verbs? See if they sound like a complete unit when you put the word here: *should* _____ or *to* _____. Check the appropriate column.

|  | Verb | Not a verb |
| --- | --- | --- |
| Sample: characteristic |  | ✗ |

UNIT 2: VERBS

*Getting started* (answers on p. 41)

1. defend
2. include
3. largest
4. how
5. learn

*More practice* (answers on the website)

6. sightsee
7. unbelievably
8. look
9. grow
10. ambitious

## Test yourself 7.2

Underline the verbs in these phrases. Test each word to see if it sounds like a complete unit when you put the word here: *should* _____ or *to* _____.
Sample: should really think

*Getting started* (answers on p. 41)

1. must not worry
2. might keep
3. wish for peace
4. may sometimes cook
5. will travel

*More practice* (answers on the website)

6. can usually sleep late
7. won't go home
8. would like guidance
9. could never build
10. shall do

# Lesson 8: The verb base

Sometimes a verb changes its form. Let's look at the following sentences. The verb is underlined in each one.
1. John should study.
2. John studied.
3. John is studying.
4. John studies.

You certainly can't say, *John should studied, or John to studied, so how do we know that studied is a verb? To test the word, you have to see if it can follow should or to in a different form, not necessarily in the form that you see in a particular sentence. For example, if you see John studied, ask yourself if there's a different form of studied that can follow should or to. In this case there is: John should study or John decided to study. So study and all its forms are verbs. The form of the verb that follows should or to is called the base form or infinitive **form**. The term infinitive is used to refer either to the base form alone (for example, study), or to the to + base form (for example, to study).

Let's put each of these verbs into its base form. The base form is underlined.
5. working: (should, to) work
6. believed: (should, to) believe
7. written: (should, to) write
8. wore: (should, to) wear
9. throws: (should, to) throw

## Test yourself 8.1

Put each of the verbs below into its base form. Simply find the form that follows *should* or *to*.
Sample: grew: grow

*Getting started* (answers on p. 41)
1. wrote:
2. talking:
3. thought:
4. considered:
5. seen:

*More practice* (answers on the website)
6. investigates:
7. spoken:
8. married:
9. decides:
10. found:

## Test yourself 8.2

Which of the following words are verbs? You may have to put some into their base form in order to be sure. Remember also that a verb usually indicates an action.

|  | Verb | Not a verb |
|---|---|---|
| Sample: flew | ✗ | |

## UNIT 2: VERBS

*Getting started* (answers on p. 41)

1. danced
2. sofa
3. large
4. gave
5. stares

*More practice* (answers on the website)

6. pushed
7. goodness
8. at
9. carries
10. them

## Test yourself 8.3

Underline the verbs in each of the sentences below, using the *should* or *to* tests to help you. You may have to put some verbs into their base forms in order to be sure. Remember also that a verb usually indicates an action.
Sample: She grabbed his arm.

*Getting started* (answers on p. 41)

1. The host greeted us cordially.
2. She should say that again.
3. Jonathan walked over to the car.
4. He washes dishes every evening.
5. You can't speak Vietnamese.

*More practice* (answers on the website)

6. My neighbor flew to Chicago.
7. The children wanted some candy.
8. Tomorrow we might go to the museum.
9. The censor usually objects to the same seven words.
10. In the afternoon I bought a present for my son.

# Lesson 9: Action verbs and linking verbs

The verbs we have looked at so far, such as *go*, *sing*, and *revise*, all indicate actions. In fact, they're called **action verbs**. However, there are other verbs which don't indicate actions. These are most commonly called **linking verbs**. One example of such a verb is the word *seem*, as in the sentences, *You seem tired*, *They've seemed busy lately*. Don't worry, though: *seem* still follows our *should* or *to* rules: *Harry should seem surprised at times*; *You don't want to seem arrogant, do you?* So even though *seem* isn't indicating an action, it's easy to identify it as a verb. Other examples of linking verbs are *resemble* and *become*. Linking verbs express a relationship between the noun or pronoun that comes before the linking verb and whatever follows it. (For pronouns, see Unit 7.)

## Test yourself 9.1

Which of the following words are verbs? See if each sounds like a complete unit when you put the word here: *should* _____ or *to* _____. Check the appropriate column. All the verbs will be linking verbs. You may have to put some in their base form to be sure.

|  | Verb | Not a verb |
|---|---|---|
| Sample: appear | **x** |  |

***Getting started*** (answers on p. 42)

1. tasted
2. friendly
3. shady
4. be
5. got

***More practice*** (answers on the website)

6. look
7. huge
8. seven
9. ocean
10. sound

## Test yourself 9.2

Underline the verbs in these sentences. Test each word to see if it sounds like a complete unit when you put the word here: *should* _____ or *to* _____. All the verbs will be linking verbs. You may have to put some in their base form to be sure.
Sample: She <u>looked</u> happy.

***Getting started*** (answers on p. 42)

1. Barry will feel awful about it.
2. Melissa resembles her mother.
3. Zack sounded extremely angry.
4. The fish tasted undercooked.
5. You were not home early.

***More practice*** (answers on the website)

6. The final exam proved difficult.
7. That dinner smells so good!
8. The firefighters remain at the station all night long.
9. They stayed indoors throughout their ordeal.
10. By noon the weather turned nice.

# UNIT 2: VERBS

The most common linking verb is the verb *be*, often called the copula. You can see different forms of the verb *be* in the following sentences.
1. I am happy.
2. You are happy.
3. He is happy.
4. I was happy.
5. You were happy.
6. I have been happy.
7. He is being happy.

Notice how different these forms are from the base form of *be*. In fact, *be* is the most irregular verb in the English language: it has more forms than any other verb. But you can still use the *should* or *to* test to identify *be* as a verb: *You should be happy, They decided to be happy.* For convenience, the forms of *be* are indicated in *Quick tip* 9.1.

> **Quick tip 9.1**
>
> The forms of the irregular verb *be* are: *am, are, is, was, were, be, been, being.*

Note that *be* and *become* are two different verbs. Here are the forms of *become*: *become, becomes, became, becoming.*

## Test yourself 9.3

Underline the forms of *be* in each of the sentences below. Some sentences may contain more than one form of *be*.
Sample: It is a privilege to meet you.

**Getting started** (answers on p. 42)
1. Paul was in power at that moment.
2. They are absolutely correct in their thinking.
3. Your suitcases were in the overhead compartment during the flight.
4. Christina has been wanting to go to Europe for a long time.
5. What is wrong with being a good student?

**More practice** (answers on the website)
6. The situation is getting out of hand.
7. My niece wants to be a psychiatrist when she grows up.
8. The problem is being corrected as we speak.
9. History might be being made right now.
10. I am happy to show you around town.

Often, forms of the verb *be* are said and written as contractions, as in these sentences:
8. I'm happy. (verb = am)
9. He's happy. (verb = is)
10. We're happy. (verb = are)
11. He's being happy. (verb = is)

These are all still sentences with *be*.
For more on the verb *be*, see Lessons 34 and 35.

## Test yourself 9.4

Underline the forms of *be* in each of the sentences below. Some will be written as contractions.
Sample: It's unusual to see rain at this time of the year.

*Lesson 9: Action verbs and linking verbs*

***Getting started*** (answers on p. 42)
1. They're usually home by now.
2. Are you worried about anything?
3. I heard that the flight was late.
4. We're honored by your presence.
5. It's too bad that the Yankees lost last night.

***More practice*** (answers on the website)
6. I think she's my husband's new boss.
7. The tyrant will certainly be accused of crimes against humanity.
8. You're a real good friend.
9. I'm afraid to tell you the truth.
10. It has been far too long since we last saw each other.

## Test yourself 9.5

Which of these words is a verb? See if it sounds like a complete unit when you put the word here: *should* _____ or *to* _____. Check the appropriate column. Some of the verbs are linking verbs and some are action verbs. All the verbs will be in their base forms.

|  | Verb | Not a verb |
|---|---|---|
| Sample: run | **x** |  |

***Getting started*** (answers on p. 42)
1. resemble
2. become
3. this
4. be
5. new

***More practice*** (answers on the website)
6. although
7. search
8. grow
9. without
10. really

## Test yourself 9.6

Which of these words is a verb? You may have to put some in their base forms in order to be sure. Some are linking verbs.

|  | Verb | Not a verb |
|---|---|---|
| Sample: orange |  | **x** |

***Getting started*** (answers on p. 42)
1. appeared
2. attends
3. whenever
4. was
5. heard

***More practice*** (answers on the website)
6. did
7. you
8. living
9. completes
10. eraser

## Test yourself 9.7

Underline the verb in each of the following sentences. You may have to put some in their base forms and test each word with *should* or *to* in order to be sure of your answer. Each sentence has only one verb. The verbs in this exercise are all action verbs.
Sample: He <u>bakes</u> cookies for his son's birthday.

# UNIT 2: VERBS

***Getting started*** (answers on p. 43)

1. The car spun out of control.
2. Don't talk during the movie.
3. The doctor tied a strip of gauze around her hand.
4. Maxine spent too much money.
5. They saw the play last Sunday.

***More practice*** (answers on the website)

6. Molly received a reply to her letter.
7. He ate on the stoop of the front porch.
8. Grandma held the kitten in her lap.
9. She never says anything.
10. They wash the windows regularly.

## Test yourself 9.8

Identify the verb in each of the following sentences. You may have to put some in their base forms and test each word with *should* or *to* in order to be sure of your answer. Each sentence has only one verb. The verbs in this exercise will be either action or linking verbs.
Sample: Bridget spent hours in the dusty old bookstore.

***Getting started*** (answers on p. 43)

1. That was the best meal in the world.
2. I understand your point.
3. Maybe they know each other well.
4. She is from Wisconsin.
5. Those flowers smell heavenly.

***More practice*** (answers on the website)

6. It seemed late.
7. Johnny packed all our things.
8. Mother is always right about that.
9. She went down to the basement.
10. I felt wonderful about my decision.

How can you determine if a verb is being used as an action verb or a linking verb? There are a number of differences between them. One way is to think of a linking verb as an equal sign (=). For example:

12. Harry resembles his brother.
    Harry = his brother.
13. You are bored.
    You = bored.
14. That strange looking vegetable tastes awful.
    That strange looking vegetable = awful.

*Resembles*, *are*, and *tastes* are each being used here as linking verbs.

Another way to identify a linking verb is to see if you can substitute a form of *be* for it, and leave the meaning basically the same. For example, take the sentence *John seems interested in the conversation*. We can substitute a form of *be*, specifically, *is*, for *seems*: *John is interested in the conversation*. Thus, *seems* is a linking verb in the sentence *John seems interested in the conversation*. Take a look at some more examples.

15. After a while, the hotel became dingy.
    After a while, the hotel was dingy.
16. Annie and Janine look surprised.
    Annie and Janine are surprised.

*Lesson 9: Action verbs and linking verbs*

    17. Although in his eighties, he remains youthful-looking.
        Although in his eighties, he is youthful-looking.
Thus, *became*, *look*, and *remains* are being used as linking verbs in these sentences. Remember that *be* and its forms can also be used as linking verbs. While *Quick tip* 9.2 below isn't foolproof, it will usually help you identify whether a verb is an action or linking verb.

> **Quick tip 9.2**
>
> If you can substitute a form of *be* for a verb and the meaning of the sentence is basically the same, the verb is probably being used as a linking verb. The verb *be* and its forms are also linking verbs.

    Another way to identify a linking verb is to see if you can substitute a form of the word *seem* for it, and leave the meaning basically the same. For example, in the sentence, *The hot shower felt soothing*, we can substitute a form of *seem* for *felt*, and leave the sentence largely unchanged: *The hot shower seemed soothing*. Note the following examples:
    18a. After a while, the hotel became dingy.
    18b. After a while, the hotel seemed dingy.
    19a. Annie and Janine look surprised.
    19b. Annie and Janine seem surprised.
    20a. Although in his eighties, he remains youthful-looking.
    20b. Although in his eighties, he seems youthful-looking.
Thus, *became*, *look*, and *remains* are being used as linking verbs in these sentences. Again, while *Quick tip* 9.3 below also isn't foolproof, it will help you identify whether a verb is an action or linking verb.

> **Quick tip 9.3**
>
> If you can substitute a form of *seem* for a verb and the meaning of the sentence is basically the same, the verb is probably being used as a linking verb.

## Test yourself 9.9

Decide if the underlined verbs in the sentences below are action or linking verbs. In this exercise, if it's a form of *be*, it's being used as a linking verb. If it's not a form of *be*, use the *be* or *seem* substitution tests to see if the verb is being used as a linking verb.

|  | Action | Linking |
|---|---|---|
| Sample: She laughed at all his jokes. | ✗ |  |

***Getting started*** (answers on p. 43)

1. The Czar was a person of high rank.
2. That dog barks a lot.
3. Mr. Kelly watched the traffic below his window.
4. You have been a terrific friend to me over the years.
5. I love the way the pillows feel so cozy in this hotel.

# UNIT 2: VERBS

*More practice* (answers on the website)

6. Jimmy is always eager to answer any questions.
7. Finding a healthy meal on the menu proved easy.
8. He's not as smart as he led me to believe.
9. We could hear the neighbors arguing for hours.
10. That sounds good to me.

## Test yourself 9.10

Underline the verb in each sentence below and decide if it's being used as an action or linking verb. In this exercise, if the verb is a form of *be*, it's being used as a linking verb. If it's not a form of *be*, use the *be* or *seem* substitution tests to see if the verb is being used as a linking verb.

|  | Action | Linking |
|---|---|---|
| Sample: The policeman gave him a ticket. | ✗ |  |

*Getting started* (answers on p. 43)

1. They became best friends.
2. It is not nearly the same as mine.
3. Unfortunately, I forgot your birthday this year.
4. I went to the corner bakery.
5. Mark remains a legend to this day.

*More practice* (answers on the website)

6. Trigonometry bores me.
7. Babies often get hungry.
8. No one got a C on the midterm exam.
9. It's much ado about nothing.
10. He made such a fuss over a minor mistake.

---

Hopefully you now have a good sense of the difference between action and linking verbs. However, there are some verbs that can be used as either an action verb or a linking verb, depending on the sentence that it's in. Compare, for example, the following two sentences with *feel*:

21. Mary felt tired.
22. Mary felt the softness of the material.

In sentence 21, *felt* is being used as a linking verb. Note that *Mary = tired*; *Mary is tired*, *Mary seems tired* all make sense here. In sentence 22, Mary is doing an action. Also, one can't think of it as: *\*Mary = the softness of the material*, *\*Mary was the softness of the material*, or *\*Mary seemed the softness of the material*. That is, thinking of *felt* as an equal sign or substituting a form of *be* or *seem* for *felt* clearly doesn't work here. Thus, in sentence 22, *felt* is being used as an action verb.

*Lesson 9: Action verbs and linking verbs*

Here are a few more examples:
23. The dinner at that restaurant <u>tasted</u> delicious. (linking verb)
    (The dinner at that restaurant was delicious.)
24. I <u>tasted</u> the soup. (action verb)
    (*I was the soup.)
25. The flowers <u>smelled</u> heavenly. (linking verb)
    (The flowers are heavenly.)
26. She <u>smelled</u> the fire before she saw it. (action verb)
    (*She was the fire before she saw it.)

## Test yourself 9.11

Underline the verb in each sentence below and decide if it's being used as an action or linking verb.

|  | Action | Linking |
|---|---|---|
| Sample: The crowd <u>grew</u> angry. |  | ✗ |

*Getting started* (answers on p. 43)

1. He grew potatoes on his farm.
2. I looked at the mess all around me.
3. Stephen looks happy today.
4. In reality, exceptions rarely prove the rule.
5. Learning the rule proved difficult.

*More practice* (answers on the website)

6. I got nervous before my blood test.
7. I got a spasm in my arm.
8. The idea of having a pizza sounds real good.
9. Last night a burglar sounded the alarm.
10. You rarely become a star overnight.

---

### To enhance your understanding

Another important difference between action and linking verbs is that a linking verb can be followed by just an adjective, while an action verb cannot:

27. She <u>is</u> tired. (*Tired* is an adjective.)
28. The mayor <u>looked</u> victorious. (*Victorious* is an adjective.)
29. *She <u>washed</u> tired.
30. *The mayor <u>voted</u> victorious.

As you can see, *is* and *looked* are linking verbs in these sentences; *washed* and *voted* are action verbs. However, since we haven't yet talked about adjectives (see Lesson 16), just keep this in mind as another difference between the two types of verbs.

# UNIT 2: VERBS

> **To further enhance your understanding**
> Compare the following two sentences:
> 31a. She looked careful. (*careful* is an adjective)
> 31b. She looked carefully. (*carefully* is an adverb)
> Can you sense the difference? In sentence 31a the verb *looked* is a linking verb, followed by the adjective *careful*; the basic meaning of the sentence is *She looked like she was a careful person*. In contrast, in sentence 31b *looked* is an action verb, followed by the adverb *carefully* (adverbs will be discussed in Lesson 27); the basic meaning of this sentence is *She looked around in a careful manner*. Quick tip 9.4 identifies yet another difference between linking verbs and action verbs.

> **Quick tip 9.4**
>
> Linking verbs are followed or modified by adjectives, while action verbs are followed or modified by adverbs.

## Test yourself 9.12 – Grand finale

If you can do this exercise, you've achieved a basic understanding of nouns and verbs.

In each sentence below, underline the nouns and put a squiggly line under each verb. Each sentence has only one verb but may have more than one noun.

Sample: The judges were unanimous in their decision.

*Getting started* (answers on p. 43)

1. Their daughter announced her engagement later.
2. The surgeon washed his hands.
3. The pianist was diligent.
4. The young boy gritted his teeth.
5. Her assistant is always late.

*More practice* (answers on the website)

6. The mayor explained his position.
7. The train came early.
8. Three other customers placed orders that day.
9. Her friend was helpful.
10. That hot meal tastes great.

# Lesson 10: Transitive and intransitive verbs

Take a look at the following questions, each with an action verb.
1. What did you write?
2. Who did you annoy?
3. What did you throw?

These are all perfectly fine questions and easy to answer, e.g. *I wrote a letter, I annoyed my neighbor, I threw a ball*.

Now compare the first group of questions to the next group, each of which also has an action verb.
4. *What did you *sleep*?
5. *What did you *die*?
6. *Who did you *arrive*?

These questions are all strange and can't really be answered. That's because the verbs in this second group are verbs that do not act on anything.

Thus, you can see that there are two kinds of verbs. One kind, such as *write*, *annoy*, and *throw*, acts upon something. The noun (or noun phrase; see Lesson 28) that the verb acts upon is called the **direct object** of the sentence. (You'll learn more about direct objects in Lesson 39.) Those verbs that act on something are called **transitive** verbs. Typically, in statements, a transitive verb is followed by the noun (or noun phrase) that it is acting upon.

Other verbs, such as *sleep*, *die*, and *arrive*, do not act upon something. In fact, these verbs can't have a direct object. Notice that you can't say, for example: *I usually sleep the dog*, *They'll arrive the book*. Those verbs that do not act on something and appear in sentences that do not have a direct object are called **intransitive** verbs.

> **Quick tip 10.1**
>
> Action verbs that act upon something are called transitive verbs. Action verbs that do not act upon something are called intransitive verbs.

> **Quick tip 10.2**
>
> If a verb (in any of its forms) can be put in one of the following slots, it is transitive: (a) What did you _____? (b) Who did you _____? If a verb cannot be put in one of these slots, it is intransitive.

So, which of the following verbs are transitive and which intransitive?
7. What did you discover?
8. *What did you struggle?
9. Who did you meet?
10. *What did you laugh?

Since sentences 7 and 9 are fine questions, *discover* and *meet* are transitive verbs. Since sentences 8 and 10 are not acceptable questions, *struggle* and *laugh* are intransitive verbs. Note

# UNIT 2: VERBS

that although you can say something like, *What did you struggle with?* or, *What did you laugh at?*, you can't ask the questions as they are stated above, and so the verbs are intransitive.

There's also another way to decide if a verb is transitive or intransitive:

> **Quick tip 10.3**
>
> If a verb (in one of its forms) can be put in one of the following slots, it is transitive:
> (a) He _____ something. (b) He _____ someone.

> **Quick tip 10.4**
>
> If a verb (in one of its forms) can be put in the following slot, it is intransitive:
> He _____.

Let's use these *Quick tips* to decide which of the following verbs are transitive and which are intransitive:
 11. He discovered something.
 12. He met someone.
 13. He struggled.
 14. He laughed.

*Quick tip* 10.3 helps identify the verb *discovered* in sentence 11 and the verb *met* in sentence 12 as transitive. *Quick tip* 10.4 helps identify the verb *struggled* in sentence 13 and the verb *laughed* in sentence 14 as intranstive.

## Test yourself 10.1

Decide if each of the verbs below is transitive or intransitive. Use *Quick tips* 9.2, 9.3 and 9.4 to help you decide.

|  | Transitive | Intransitive |
|---|---|---|
| Sample: mention | x | |

*Getting started* (answers on p. 44)

1. tell
2. rise
3. raise
4. fall
5. publish

*More practice* (answers on the website)

6. proclaim
7. vanish
8. omit
9. cry
10. remove

Now take a look at a few more sentences:
 15a. I ate.
 15b. I ate dinner.
 16a. She dances well.
 16b. She dances the tango well.
 17a. The audience left.
 17b. The audience left the theater.

*Lesson 10: Transitive and intransitive verbs*

You can see that there are verbs, such as *eat, dance,* and *leave,* that can be used as either transitive or intransitive verbs.

> **Quick tip 10.5**
>
> Some verbs can be either transitive or transitive. These can occur in both of the following slots: (a) He _____ something / someone. (b) He _____.

## Test yourself 10.2

Decide if each of the verbs below is transitive, intransitive, or either. Use *Quick tips* 10.2, 10.3, 10.4, and 10.5 to help you decide.

|  | Transitive | Intransitive | Either |
|---|---|---|---|
| Sample: play |  |  | x |

***Getting started*** (answers on p. 44)

| | Transitive | Intransitive | Either |
|---|---|---|---|
| 1. beat | | | |
| 2. cough | | | |
| 3. relax | | | |
| 4. drive | | | |
| 5. entertain | | | |

***More practice*** (answers on the website)

| | Transitive | Intransitive | Either |
|---|---|---|---|
| 6. seek | | | |
| 7. fight | | | |
| 8. profit | | | |
| 9. mention | | | |
| 10. paint | | | |

## Test yourself 10.3

In the sentences below, decide if the underlined verb is being used as a transitive or intransitive verb. Use *Quick tips* 9.2 and 9.3 to help you decide.

|  | Transitive | Intransitive |
|---|---|---|
| Sample: They played in the park. |  | x |

***Getting started*** (answers on p. 44)

| | Transitive | Intransitive |
|---|---|---|
| 1. Greg opened the newspaper. | | |
| 2. I can read it later. | | |
| 3. Don't worry! | | |
| 4. On Sundays, I usually stay at home. | | |
| 5. It's advisable to wash your hands before eating. | | |

***More practice*** (answers on the website)

| | Transitive | Intransitive |
|---|---|---|
| 6. Samantha can bake at any time of the day. | | |
| 7. When I'm tired, I complain. | | |
| 8. She ended the conversation. | | |
| 9. The athlete hit the ball. | | |
| 10. My dog licked my face playfully. | | |

# Lesson 11: Phrasal verbs

While most verbs are single words, some are **phrasal**: they contain two words. In phrasal verbs, the first word is a verb and the second word is called a particle. Here are some examples, with the phrasal verbs underlined:
1. She looked up the answer.
2. We will just drop off the files.
3. The professor pointed out the correct answer.

Notice that the meaning of a phrasal verb is often similar to the meaning of a single verb:
4. She looked up the answer.
   She researched the answer.
5. We will just drop off the files.
   We will just deliver the files.
6. The professor pointed out the correct answer.
   The professor identified the correct answer.

> **Quick tip 11.1**
>
> If you can substitute a single verb for a verb and the word following it, you probably have a phrasal verb. For example, you can say, She pointed out the truth to us or She showed the truth to us. Point out is a phrasal verb.

We can also still identify phrasal verbs using our *to* ____ or *should* ____ Quick tips:

| to look up | should look up |
| to warm up | should warm up |
| to point out | should point out |

## Test yourself 11.1

Each of the sentences below contains a phrasal verb. Underline the phrasal verb, using the verb substitution tip and the *to* ____ and *should* ____ tips to help you.
Sample: The lecturer summed up his main points.

**Getting started** (answers on p. 44)

1. He fixed up the lighting in the hall.
2. They read over the document many times.
3. You dream up the most amazing things.
4. Ron takes out the garbage every Monday night.
5. I will pay off my mortgage in fifteen years.

*Lesson 11: Phrasal verbs*

***More practice*** (answers on the website)

6. Yesterday, the company's president handed in her resignation.
7. She took over the entire operation.
8. Unfortunately, the buyer of my property blew off the deal.
9. It is obvious that she cooked up the whole story.
10. You bring up an interesting point.

---

In many cases, the two parts of a phrasal verb, the verb and its particle, can be separated:
    7. She looked the answer up.
    8. We will just drop the files off.
    9. The professor pointed the correct answer out.
Even when the two parts are separated, it's still a phrasal, or multi-word, verb. When you can separate the two parts in this way, you know that you've got a phrasal verb.

> **Quick tip 11.2**
>
> If you can move a particle away from its verb, you have a phrasal verb. For example, since you can say both *She looked up the answer* and *She looked the answer up*, *look up* is a phrasal verb.

## Test yourself 11.2

Underline the phrasal verbs in each of the sentences below. The particle will not necessarily be next to its verb.
Sample: The students will hand their assignment in tomorrow.

***Getting started*** (answers on p. 44)

1. Mr. Parker helped out his neighbors.
2. You should call the agency up.
3. Those children put on a show.
4. What brought this reaction about?
5. The hurricane tore the roofs of many houses off.

***More practice*** (answers on the website)

6. The first member of the relay team passed off the baton successfully.
7. The herdsman gathered all his sheep in.
8. Debbie kept up her grades in graduate school.
9. I took my glasses off quickly.
10. Last month the bank signed the deed over to me.

---

In some cases, a particle cannot be separated from its verb:
    10. She asked for the receptionist.
    11. The lawyer objected to the defendant's statement.
    12. He will look into the judge's decision.

# UNIT 2: VERBS

In these cases, you cannot say:
    13. *She <u>asked</u> the receptionist <u>for</u>.
    14. *The lawyer <u>objected</u> the defendant's statement <u>to</u>.
    15. *He will <u>look</u> the judge's decision <u>into</u>.

So *Quick tip* 11.2 is not useful in these cases; you have to rely on the verb substitution test and the *to* and *should* tests.

## Test yourself 11.3

Some of the sentences below contain a one word verb and some contain a phrasal verb. Underline the one word verb or phrasal verb in each sentence.
Sample: They <u>owed</u> her a lot of money.

***Getting started*** (answers on p. 44)

1. Eat up your dinner!
2. The girls will put the puzzles away.
3. I understand that concept.
4. Birds fly south for the winter.
5. The elderly woman got off the bus with great difficulty.

***More practice*** (answers on the website)

6. We ate out last night.
7. The show ran far too long.
8. They checked out the scenery around their hotel.
9. The pitcher threw the batter out in the eighth inning.
10. The butcher opened his store up at 7 A.M.

## To enhance your understanding

Take a look at these groups of sentences:
    16. She <u>looked up</u> the answer.    She <u>looked</u> the answer <u>up</u>.
          *She <u>looked up</u> it.    She <u>looked</u> it <u>up</u>.
    17. We will just <u>drop off</u> the children. We will just <u>drop</u> the children <u>off</u>.
          *We will just <u>drop off</u> them.    We will just <u>drop</u> them <u>off</u>.
    18. He <u>pointed out</u> the other girl.    He <u>pointed</u> the other girl <u>out</u>.
          *He <u>pointed out</u> her.    He <u>pointed</u> her <u>out</u>.

As you can see, in some cases (those with an asterisk), a particle cannot be next to its verb; the two parts must be separated. As a matter of fact, this is true in all of those cases where the direct object of the verb (what the verb is acting upon) is one of the following words: *me, you, him, her, it, us, them*. You might recognize these words as pronouns. You'll learn about these pronouns in Lesson 21, about direct objects in Lesson 39, and more about verbs and their particles in Lesson 30.

# Answer keys: *Test yourself, Getting started* questions – Unit 2

## Test yourself 7.1

|   | Verb | Not a verb |
|---|---|---|
| 1. defend | ✗ |   |
| 2. include | ✗ |   |
| 3. largest |   | ✗ |
| 4. how |   | ✗ |
| 5. learn | ✗ |   |

## Test yourself 7.2

1. must not <u>worry</u>
2. might <u>keep</u>
3. <u>wish</u> for peace
4. may sometimes <u>cook</u>
5. will <u>travel</u>

## Test yourself 8.1

1. wrote: <u>write</u>
2. talking: <u>talk</u>
3. thought: <u>think</u>
4. considered: <u>consider</u>
5. seen: <u>see</u>

## Test yourself 8.2

|   | Verb | Not a verb |
|---|---|---|
| 1. danced | ✗ |   |
| 2. sofa |   | ✗ |
| 3. large |   | ✗ |
| 4. gave | ✗ |   |
| 5. stares | ✗ |   |

## Test yourself 8.3

1. The host <u>greeted</u> us cordially.
2. She should <u>say</u> that again.
3. Jonathan <u>walked</u> over to the car.
4. He <u>washes</u> dishes every evening.
5. You can't <u>speak</u> Vietnamese.

# UNIT 2: VERBS

## Test yourself 9.1

|   | Verb | Not a verb |
|---|---|---|
| 1. tasted | ✗ |  |
| 2. friendly |  | ✗ |
| 3. shady |  | ✗ |
| 4. be | ✗ |  |
| 5. got | ✗ |  |

## Test yourself 9.2

1. Barry will <u>feel</u> awful about it.
2. Melissa <u>resembles</u> her mother.
3. Zack <u>sounded</u> extremely angry.
4. The fish <u>tasted</u> undercooked.
5. You <u>were</u> not home early.

## Test yourself 9.3

1. Paul <u>was</u> in power at that moment.
2. They <u>are</u> absolutely correct in their thinking.
3. Your suitcases <u>were</u> in the overhead compartment during the flight.
4. Christina has <u>been</u> wanting to go to Europe for a long time.
5. What <u>is</u> wrong with <u>being</u> a good student?

## Test yourself 9.4

1. They'<u>re</u> usually home by now.
2. <u>Are</u> you worried about anything?
3. I heard that the flight <u>was</u> late.
4. We'<u>re</u> honored by your presence.
5. It'<u>s</u> too bad that the Yankees lost last night.

## Test yourself 9.5

|   | Verb | Not a verb |
|---|---|---|
| 1. resemble | ✗ |  |
| 2. become | ✗ |  |
| 3. this |  | ✗ |
| 4. be | ✗ |  |
| 5. new |  | ✗ |

## Test yourself 9.6

|   | Verb | Not a verb |
|---|---|---|
| 1. appeared | ✗ |  |
| 2. attends | ✗ |  |
| 3. whenever |  | ✗ |
| 4. was | ✗ |  |
| 5. heard | ✗ |  |

*Anwser keys: Unit 2*

## Test yourself 9.7

1. The car <u>spun</u> out of control.
2. Don't <u>talk</u> during the movie.
3. The doctor <u>tied</u> a strip of gauze around her hand.
4. Maxine <u>spent</u> too much money.
5. They <u>saw</u> the play last Sunday.

## Test yourself 9.8

1. That <u>was</u> the best meal in the world.
2. I <u>understand</u> your point.
3. Maybe they <u>know</u> each other well.
4. She <u>is</u> from Wisconsin.
5. Those flowers <u>smell</u> heavenly.

## Test yourself 9.9

|  | Action | Linking |
|---|---|---|
| 1. The Czar <u>was</u> a person of high rank. |  | x |
| 2. That dog <u>barks</u> a lot. | x |  |
| 3. Mr. Kelly <u>watched</u> the traffic below his window. | x |  |
| 4. You have <u>been</u> a terrific friend to me over the years. |  | x |
| 5. I love the way the pillows <u>feel</u> so cozy in this hotel. |  | x |

## Test yourself 9.10

|  | Action | Linking |
|---|---|---|
| 1. They <u>became</u> best friends. |  | x |
| 2. It <u>is</u> not nearly the same as mine. |  | x |
| 3. Unfortunately, I <u>forgot</u> your birthday this year. | x |  |
| 4. I <u>went</u> to the corner bakery. | x |  |
| 5. Mark <u>remains</u> a legend to this day. |  | x |

## Test yourself 9.11

|  | Action | Linking |
|---|---|---|
| 1. He <u>grew</u> potatoes on his farm. | x |  |
| 2. I <u>looked</u> at the mess all around me. | x |  |
| 3. Stephen <u>looks</u> happy today. |  | x |
| 4. In reality, exceptions rarely <u>prove</u> the rule. | x |  |
| 5. Learning the rule <u>proved</u> difficult. |  | x |

## Test yourself 9.12

1. Their <u>daughter</u> <u>announced</u> her <u>engagement</u> later.
2. The <u>surgeon</u> <u>washed</u> his <u>hands</u>.
3. The <u>pianist</u> <u>was</u> diligent.
4. The young <u>boy</u> <u>gritted</u> his <u>teeth</u>.
5. Her <u>assistant</u> <u>is</u> always late.

# UNIT 2: VERBS

## Test yourself 10.1

|  | Transitive | Intransitive |
|---|---|---|
| 1. tell | x |  |
| 2. rise |  | x |
| 3. raise | x |  |
| 4. fall |  | x |
| 5. publish | x |  |

## Test yourself 10.2

|  | Transitive | Intransitive | Either |
|---|---|---|---|
| 1. beat | x |  |  |
| 2. cough |  | x |  |
| 3. relax |  | x |  |
| 4. drive |  |  | x |
| 5. entertain |  |  | x |

## Test yourself 10.3

|  | Transitive | Intransitive |
|---|---|---|
| 1. Greg opened the newspaper. | x |  |
| 2. I can read it later. | x |  |
| 3. Don't worry! |  | x |
| 4. On Sundays, I usually stay at home. |  | x |
| 5. It's advisable to wash your hands before eating. | x |  |

## Test yourself 11.1

1. He fixed up the lighting in the hall.
2. They read over the document many times.
3. You dream up the most amazing things.
4. Ron takes out the garbage every Monday night.
5. I will pay off my mortgage in fifteen years.

## Test yourself 11.2

1. Mr. Parker helped out his neighbors.
2. You should call the agency up.
3. Those children put on a show.
4. What brought this reaction about?
5. The hurricane tore the roofs of many houses off.

## Test yourself 11.3

1. Eat up your dinner!
2. The girls will put the puzzles away.
3. I understand that concept.
4. Birds fly south for the winter.
5. The elderly woman got off the bus with great difficulty.

☞ **FOR A REVIEW EXERCISE OF THIS UNIT, SEE THE WEBSITE.**

# UNIT 3: DETERMINERS

Determiners are words that can occur directly before a noun, tell us a bit more about that noun, and introduce it. The determiners are underlined in the sentences below, with the following noun in bold:
1. I milked the **cow**.
2. It is Harry's **turn**.
3. They bought that **house**.
4. John has more **money**.

These sentences have examples of the four major types of determiners: articles, possessives, demonstratives, and quantifiers. Generally, a noun will have only one of these determiner types in front of it. We'll be discussing each of these four types in this unit, starting with articles, the easiest and most common.

# Lesson 12: Articles

How can you identify an *article*?
It doesn't get any easier than this!

> **Quick tip 12.1**
>
> There are only three articles in English: *the, a* and *an*.

Articles give us information about a noun; they indicate whether or not the noun is a specific one known to both the speaker and listener. Take a look at these examples to see what we mean:
1. I bought a red car. (The listener doesn't know anything about the red car.)
2. The red car was on sale. (The listener knows which car the speaker is talking about.)

*The* is commonly called the **definite article**; *a* and *an* are called **indefinite articles**. The definite article may be used with both singular and plural nouns, but the indefinite articles only with singular nouns, as we can see in the following examples:

| the idea | the ideas |
|---|---|
| an apple | *an apples |
| a revolution | *a revolutions |

## Test yourself 12.1

Underline the articles in each of the sentences below. A sentence may have more than one article.
Sample: We watched a video last night.

***Getting started*** (answers on p. 55)

1. The last week of the month was a busy one in the store.
2. Summer was a special time for Melissa.
3. There's an unusual idea floating around.
4. I turned a corner in the long hall.
5. A dirty spoon had fallen to the floor.

***More practice*** (answers on the website)

6. In the middle of the night, I heard a strange noise.
7. Jackie turned off the road too soon.
8. Your mother's favorite actor appeared in the show we saw last night.
9. A pear is just as tasty as an apple, as far as I am concerned.
10. The guys bought two cans of paint: an orange one and a beige one.

## Lesson 12: Articles

What's the difference between *a* and *an*? See if you notice a pattern when you look at these examples:

| a red tablecloth | an ancient right |
| a situation | an interesting message |
| a boring lecture | an intruder |

The articles *a* and *an* have the same meaning and use. The only difference between them is that *a* is used when the next word begins with a consonant sound, while *an* is used when the next word begins with a vowel sound.

> **To enhance your understanding**
> What about *a uniform* and *an hour*? Do these contradict what we've said about when to use *a* and *an*? It certainly looks like *a* is being used before a vowel, and *an* is being used before a consonant. But in fact, that's not the case. These phrases follow the rule perfectly. Remember that *a* is used when the next word begins with a consonant <u>sound</u>. The first letter of the next word doesn't matter; only its first sound matters.
> So what's the first <u>sound</u> of the word *uniform*? Say it out loud and listen carefully. You will hear that the first <u>sound</u> of the word is the sound [y], as in *yes*. We really say "y-uniform" (and also "y-unicorn," "y-usual," etc.). Since "y," a consonant, is the first sound, we use *a* before *uniform*.
> What's the first <u>sound</u> of the word *hour*? Say the word out loud, and you will notice that in fact we don't pronounce the letter "h." Rather, *hour* begins with a vowel sound, as in the word *our*, and so we say *an hour*.
> Thus, apparent exceptions, like *a uniform* and *an hour*, are not exceptions at all.

## Test yourself 12.2

For each sentence, underline each article with a <u>solid line</u>, each noun with a <u>double underline</u>, and each verb with a <u>squiggly line</u>. Some sentences have more than one article and noun; some have no article. If you can answer these questions, you have achieved a solid understanding of how to identify articles, nouns, and verbs, three of the most common parts of speech!
Sample: <u>A</u> <u><u>pilot</u></u> spoke to the <u><u>crew</u></u>.

***Getting started*** (answers on p. 55)

1. A waiter walked to the table.
2. The trainer calmed the dog down.
3. He argued about the bill for hours.
4. I usually eat a sandwich and a cookie for lunch.
5. She watches TV every night.

***More practice*** (answers on the website)

6. The train appeared suddenly.
7. Diane put the chicken in the salad.
8. The repairman did not finish his job.
9. Children like cake.
10. Nowadays Elena takes skiing lessons at least once a week.

# Lesson 13: Demonstratives

Here's another easy category. There are only four demonstratives: *this*, *that*, *these*, and *those*.

> **Quick tip 13.1**
>
> There are only four demonstratives in English: *this*, *that*, *these*, and *those*.

Notice again that, just like articles, each of these can occur directly before a noun: *this table*, *these tables*, *that idea*, *those ideas*. Demonstratives are words that "point" to something or someone.

## Test yourself 13.1

Underline the demonstrative in each of the sentences below.
Sample: <u>Those</u> performers were all also composers.

***Getting started*** (answers on p. 55)

1. You can use this book.
2. Those speeches he gave were impressive.
3. They don't speak that language.
4. Kirsten sold all these items.
5. This side of the Atlantic Ocean is more familiar to me.

***More practice*** (answers on the website)

6. She likes to listen to that song.
7. Those mistakes will catch up with Andrew one day.
8. I don't like these pictures.
9. That man is a technician.
10. Lots of people like to patronize this restaurant.

## Test yourself 13.2

Underline the determiners in the sentences below. They will be either articles or demonstratives.
Sample: There were shops selling <u>a</u> variety of <u>those</u> handmade items.

***Getting started*** (answers on p. 55)

1. On top of the pile of fabrics was a sleeping cat.
2. That leader met with the residents of the village.
3. This taxi is heading toward a large shopping mall.
4. The instructor chose a very informative textbook.
5. These pants won't fit in those drawers.

***More practice*** (answers on the website)

6. The audience is tired of all those lame jokes.
7. Once in a while I think of my childhood friends.
8. Those pedestrians better keep to the right of the main road.
9. This work is the brainchild of a madman.
10. We found this piece of paper on the top shelf of a dusty bookcase.

*Lesson 13: Demonstratives*

## Test yourself 13.3

Identify each determiner in the sentences below by underlining it with a solid line if it is a demonstrative and with a squiggly line if it is an article.
Sample: Larry is holding <u>this</u> meeting at ~the~ hotel.

***Getting started*** (answers on p. 55)

1. Are you looking for a better job?
2. That movie follows a young family after they immigrate to this country.
3. Jane met an Englishman there whom she later married.
4. The weather was so wonderful at the beach.
5. All those cups of coffee won't help you get a good night's rest.

***More practice*** (answers on the website)

6. I recognize this soccer player as a big star from Italy.
7. Playing a game of chess in this park always interests me.
8. Those students who did the exercises in the text will likely pass the final.
9. The garbage is piling up on the sidewalk.
10. This lesson is a piece of cake, isn't it?

# Lesson 14: Possessives

Possessives are words that indicate ownership or belonging. The possessives are underlined in the sentences below.
1. I sold my car.
2. Betty's neighbor is an architect.

The possessive in sentence 1 is called a possessive pronoun; the possessive in sentence 2 is called a possessive proper noun. Notice that, just like articles and demonstratives, possessive pronouns and possessive proper nouns can appear directly before a noun. We'll discuss each of these separately.

### Possessive pronouns

There are just a few possessive pronouns that function as determiners. These are commonly referred to as possessive pronouns **with determiner function** or possessive adjectives. We will call them simply determiner possessive pronouns. (For another function of possessive pronouns, see Lesson 24.)

> **Quick tip 14.1**
>
> The determiner possessive pronouns are: *my, your, his, her, its, our, their.*

### Test yourself 14.1

Underline the determiner possessive pronoun in each of the sentences below.
Sample: My school won the state championship last year.

*Getting started* (answers on p. 55)

1. His face always shows what he's thinking.
2. They go to their house in the mountains every summer.
3. It took three days for your letter to get here.
4. We liked her mother.
5. Our product is superior to what you have to offer.

*More practice* (answers on the website)

6. The price of the stock I am considering buying does not reflect its true worth.
7. Would you like to take a ride in your new car?
8. Friends, I will be counting on your votes.
9. The children went to the movies together with their father.
10. Matt does not share his feelings easily.

### Possessive proper nouns

The possessive proper nouns are underlined in this next sentence:
3. I saw Mary's cat chase Mrs. Smith's dog, which ran across Jim's yard.

*Lesson 14: Possessives*

Remember, names do not have to be names of just people. For example, *London's*, *America's*, and *IBM's* are each possessive proper nouns: *London's bridges*, *America's highways*, *IBM's products*. (See Lesson 6 to remind yourself about proper nouns.)

> **To enhance your understanding**
> While possessive proper nouns can function as determiners, possessive common nouns (see Lesson 6), for example *the girl's hat*, are considered to be adjectives. (See Lesson 16 for more about adjectives.) This is because possessive common nouns, but not possessive proper nouns, can have a determiner in front of them – keeping in mind that a noun will generally have just one determiner introducing it. See the following examples:
> 4. The girl's hat is new. (girl's = possessive common noun)
> 5. *The Mary's hat is new. (Mary's = possessive proper noun)

## Test yourself 14.2

Underline the possessive proper noun in each of the sentences below.
Sample: *Gone With the Wind's* cast was amazing.

***Getting started*** (answers on p. 56)

1. Leah's eyes met those of the man at the counter.
2. It was Harry's turn to say something.
3. They were impressed by Rome's restaurants.
4. Mickey Mouse's picture is hanging on my wall.
5. John always wanted to visit Harvard's campus.

***More practice*** (answers on the website)

6. France's soccer team lost to another team.
7. Macy's women's department is on the third floor.
8. Mrs. Johnson's office is located directly above mine.
9. After dinner, we went up to Beth's apartment.
10. I never get tired of The Beatles' songs.

## Test yourself 14.3

Underline the possessive determiner in each of the sentences below. The determiner will either be a possessive pronoun or a possessive proper noun.
Sample: Your committee is meeting tomorrow.

***Getting started*** (answers on p. 56)

1. She suggested that it was all Martin's fault.
2. Why don't you give it to your daughter?
3. That was a breathtaking view of New York's skyline.
4. He bought a souvenir for his son.
5. The Adamses did not care for their new neighbors.

***More practice*** (answers on the website)

6. The public was eagerly awaiting Congress's new energy policy.
7. My apartment is either too hot or too cold.
8. Abraham Lincoln's life was interesting.
9. Our crew prepared to dock.
10. On Thursday afternoon, the actor was practicing his lines.

## UNIT 3: DETERMINERS

### Test yourself 14.4

For each determiner below, indicate if it is an article (e.g. *the*, *an*), demonstrative (e.g. *this*, *those*), possessive pronoun (e.g. *your*, *our*), or possessive proper noun (e.g. *Mary's*, *London's*).
Sample: Law and Order's    possessive proper noun

*Getting started* (answers on p. 56)

1. their
2. an
3. George's
4. those
5. its

*More practice* (answers on the website)

6. the
7. San Francisco's
8. this
9. my
10. a

### Test yourself 14.5

Underline the determiner in each of the sentences below. It will either be an article, demonstrative, possessive pronoun, or possessive proper noun. Some sentences may contain more than one determiner.
Sample: The room contained a sofa, a chair, and, on the wall, Melinda's portrait.

*Getting started* (answers on p. 56)

1. She knew what her mother had done for the family.
2. There wasn't much information in his letters.
3. These books are clearly the best.
4. Rosa's husband put a surprise in her lunch box.
5. Jerry's uncle likes to drink a glass of wine with his dinner.

*More practice* (answers on the website)

6. This actress should get an Oscar for her performance in that movie.
7. The doctor's secretary usually walks a mile on her lunch break.
8. Those children love to take a dip in their new pool in the backyard.
9. On her way to work, Maggie's car broke down.
10. Jet Blue's crew served dinner while I was sleeping.

# Lesson 15: Quantifiers

There are words, such as *every* and *several*, that indicate amount, or quantity, and these are called quantifiers. Quantifiers can act as determiners; that is, they can come before and introduce a noun. The determiners are underlined in the following sentences:
1. All businesses need to have a budget.
2. Some people like eating eel.
3. She enjoyed few things as much as food.

Some common quantifiers are listed below:

| | | |
|---|---|---|
| all | enough | much |
| any | every | neither |
| both | few | no |
| each | little | several |
| either | most | some |

> **Quick tip 15.1**
>
> Words of quantity, quantifiers, can act as determiners and precede a noun. Some examples are: *all, some, several,* and *much.*

## Test yourself 15.1

Underline the quantifier in each of the sentences below. The quantifiers will all be from the list above.
Sample: I met several chefs at that school.

*Getting started* (answers on p. 56)

1. There is no writer who is as famous as Shakespeare.
2. Enough money was raised to build a new wing on the hospital.
3. I don't take much sugar in my coffee.
4. With little effort, I solved the crossword puzzle.
5. All experiments test hypotheses.

*More practice* (answers on the website)

6. Most professors have earned a doctorate.
7. Every noun that is human is also animate.
8. Neither option is particularly good.
9. Any man who drinks and drives puts his life in danger.
10. You leave me with few alternatives.

## Test yourself 15.2

For each determiner below, indicate if it is an article (e.g. *the, an*), demonstrative (e.g. *this, those*), possessive pronoun (e.g. *your, our*), possessive proper noun (e.g. *Mary's, London's*), or quantifier (e.g. *every, some*).
Sample: that    demonstrative

# UNIT 3: DETERMINERS

***Getting started*** (answers on p. 56)

1. Main Street's
2. your
3. few
4. those
5. the

***More practice*** (answers on the website)

6. its
7. both
8. Madrid's
9. several
10. an

## Test yourself 15.3

Underline the determiner in each of the sentences below. It will either be an <u>article</u> (e.g. *the*, *an*), <u>demonstrative</u> (e.g. *this*, *those*), <u>possessive pronoun</u> (e.g. *your*, *our*), <u>possessive proper noun</u> (e.g. *Mary's*, *London's*), or <u>quantifier</u> (e.g. *few, most*). Some sentences may contain more than one determiner.

Sample: <u>Joan's</u> mother valued <u>her</u> efforts.

***Getting started*** (answers on p. 57)

1. Chicago's architecture is diverse.
2. I know that man and his wife.
3. She packed several dresses into her suitcase.
4. He had traveled to few places over the years.
5. Each child at the party brought a gift.

***More practice*** (answers on the website)

6. Let's not forget those messages.
7. Every time we eat out, you order several appetizers.
8. Any man who is my friend's enemy is no friend of mine.
9. I bought these strawberries at her uncle's grocery store.
10. This event wasn't much fun.

# Answer keys: *Test yourself, Getting started* questions – Unit 3

### Test yourself 12.1

1. The last week of the month was a busy one in the store.
2. Summer was a special time for Melissa.
3. There's an unusual idea floating around.
4. I turned a corner in the long hall.
5. A dirty spoon had fallen to the floor.

### Test yourself 12.2

1. A waiter walked to the table.
2. The trainer calmed the dog down.
3. He argued about the bill for hours.
4. I usually eat a sandwich and a cookie for lunch.
5. She watches TV every night.

### Test yourself 13.1

1. You can use this book.
2. Those speeches he gave were impressive.
3. They don't speak that language.
4. Kirsten sold all these items.
5. This side of the Atlantic Ocean is more familiar to me.

### Test yourself 13.2

1. On top of the pile of fabrics was a sleeping cat.
2. That leader met with the residents of the village.
3. This taxi is heading toward a large shopping mall.
4. The instructor chose a very informative textbook.
5. These pants won't fit in those drawers.

### Test yourself 13.3

1. Are you looking for a better job?
2. That movie follows a young family after they immigrate to this country.
3. Jane met an Englishman there whom she later married.
4. The weather was so wonderful at the beach.
5. All those cups of coffee won't help you get a good night's rest.

### Test yourself 14.1

1. His face always shows what he's thinking.
2. They go to their house in the mountains every summer.

## UNIT 3: DETERMINERS

3. It took three days for <u>your</u> letter to get here.
4. We liked <u>her</u> mother.
5. <u>Our</u> product is superior to what you have to offer.

### Test yourself 14.2

1. <u>Leah's</u> eyes met those of the man at the counter.
2. It was <u>Harry's</u> turn to say something.
3. They were impressed by <u>Rome's</u> restaurants.
4. <u>Mickey Mouse's</u> picture is hanging on my wall.
5. John always wanted to visit <u>Harvard's</u> campus.

### Test yourself 14.3

1. She suggested that it was all <u>Martin's</u> fault.
2. Why don't you give it to <u>your</u> daughter?
3. That was a breathtaking view of <u>New York's</u> skyline.
4. He bought a souvenir for <u>his</u> son.
5. The Adamses did not care for <u>their</u> new neighbors.

### Test yourself 14.4

1. their — possessive pronoun
2. an — article
3. George's — possessive proper noun
4. those — demonstrative
5. its — possessive pronoun

### Test yourself 14.5

1. She knew what <u>her</u> mother had done for <u>the</u> family.
2. There wasn't much information in <u>his</u> letters.
3. <u>These</u> books are clearly <u>the</u> best.
4. <u>Rosa's</u> husband put <u>a</u> surprise in <u>her</u> lunch box.
5. <u>Jerry's</u> uncle likes to drink <u>a</u> glass of wine with <u>his</u> dinner.

### Test yourself 15.1

1. There is <u>no</u> writer who is as famous as Shakespeare.
2. <u>Enough</u> money was raised to build a new wing on the hospital.
3. I don't take <u>much</u> sugar in my coffee.
4. With <u>little</u> effort, I solved the crossword puzzle.
5. <u>All</u> experiments test hypotheses.

### Test yourself 15.2

1. Main Street's — possessive proper noun
2. your — possessive pronoun
3. few — quantifier
4. those — demonstrative
5. the — article

## Test yourself 15.3

1. <u>Chicago's</u> architecture is diverse.
2. I know <u>that</u> man and <u>his</u> wife.
3. She packed <u>several</u> dresses into <u>her</u> suitcase.
4. He had traveled to <u>few</u> places over <u>the</u> years.
5. <u>Each</u> child at <u>the</u> party brought <u>a</u> gift.

☞ **FOR A REVIEW EXERCISE OF THIS UNIT, SEE THE WEBSITE.**

## UNIT 4: ADJECTIVES

# Lesson 16: Identifying adjectives

An adjective is a word that refers to a characteristic of a noun. How can you identify an adjective?

If you can put a word between *the* and a noun (like *boy*, or *idea*), then that word is an adjective.

> **Quick tip 16.1**
>
> If you can put a word between *the* and a noun (for example, *the \_\_\_\_\_ boy*), then that word is an adjective.

For example, since we can say *the tall boy*, *tall* is an adjective. Similarly, we can say *the silly boy*, *the interesting boy*, and *the young boy*. Therefore, *silly*, *interesting*, and *young* are all adjectives.

A number of adjectives, all used in the phrase *the \_\_\_\_\_ boy* are listed below. The adjectives are underlined:

1. the brilliant boy
2. the embarrassed boy
3. the blonde boy
4. the hungry boy
5. the delightful boy

Compare these phrases to *\*the very boy*, *\*the a boy*, and *\*the talk boy*. *Very*, *a*, and *talk* are not adjectives.

What do adjectives actually do? Adjectives always tell us something about a noun. Another way of saying this is that they modify a noun. In the phrases we've just looked at, the underlined adjectives tell us something about, or modify, the noun *boy*.

### Test yourself 16.1

Which of the following words are adjectives? See if they sound right when you put them here: *the \_\_\_\_\_ thing*. Check the appropriate column.

|  | Adjective | Not an adjective |
|---|---|---|
| Sample: have |  | x |

**Getting started** (answers on p. 63)

1. yellow
2. wonderful
3. these
4. quickly
5. unreliable

**More practice** (answers on the website)

6. is
7. pure
8. on
9. creative
10. almost

*Lesson 16: Identifying adjectives*

## Test yourself 16.2

Underline the adjectives in the sentences below. In each case, the adjective will be between *the* and a noun. A sentence may have more than one adjective.
Sample: She has been the strong leader of this company for years.

***Getting started*** (answers on p. 63)

1. The strange robots marched towards the city.
2. It was the last day of school.
3. We tugged at the enormous gate.
4. The billowing smoke alerted us to the fire.
5. The sudden sandstorm forced the surprised bathers to flee the beach.

***More practice*** (answers on the website)

6. She received the exciting news in the noisy restaurant.
7. The blind beggar was sitting at the busy corner.
8. Jeremy did not get the subtle humor of the play.
9. The poor people of the world outnumber the rich ones.
10. Keep your hands off the hot stove!

As we've said, a good way to decide if a word is an adjective is to see if it can be placed between *the* and a noun. But that doesn't mean that that's the only place where an adjective can occur; it's just a way to test a word to see if it's an adjective.

Here are some sentences where the adjective is in a different place. In each case, the adjective is underlined.

6. He is a tall boy.
7. My best friend loves chocolate cake.
8. The house had a low roof.
9. Large cars are harder to drive than small cars.

Let's make sure that each of the underlined words above passes the adjective test, that is, that it can appear between *the* and a noun.

10. tall: the tall boy
11. best: the best movie
12. chocolate: the chocolate bar
13. low: the low ceiling
14. large: the large window
15. small: the small window.

As you can see, each of these words passes the adjective test. Notice also that each of these words describes a characteristic of a noun.

## Test yourself 16.3

Use the adjective test to find the adjectives in each of the sentences below. A sentence may have more than one adjective.
Sample: It took a long time to arrive at our next destination.

# UNIT 4: ADJECTIVES

*Getting started* (answers on p. 63)

1. Evenings were a special time for the family.
2. The next week was a busy one in the store.
3. There's an unusual idea floating around.
4. I turned a corner in the long hall.
5. A dirty fork had fallen to the floor.

*More practice* (answers on the website)

6. I wrote a boring letter.
7. Mary's younger brother was already there.
8. The American flag was behind Edward's desk.
9. I could see his face in the red light from the exit sign.
10. We gathered the important facts from those dusty books.

What do you notice about the underlined adjectives in the phrases below?
16. the delicious rich cake
17. my tall, red-haired, entertaining friend
18. a bright, colorful, blue, striped pattern

As you can see, a noun can have more than one adjective modifying it. In fact, there is no limit to the number of adjectives that can modify a noun (except the patience and tolerance of the listener!).

## Test yourself 16.4

Underline the adjectives in each of the sentences below. Some of the nouns will be modified by more than one adjective.
Sample: She ate all the crisp, crunchy chips.

*Getting started* (answers on p. 63)

1. They went off to see an old, gloomy, historic mansion in southern England.
2. She had anticipated his sudden arrival.
3. Angela ignored his annoying, persistent questions.
4. I must get rid of my decrepit, banged-up little old car.
5. We wouldn't want to cross this wide, busy street, would we?

*More practice* (answers on the website)

6. You should heed the advice of wise men and women.
7. Wild animals can be dangerous.
8. The lovely young lady read one of her favorite novels on her comfortable sofa.
9. Why did you buy this outdated computer in the first place?
10. The Dodgers' frustrated manager benched his brash young pitcher.

Remember that sometimes a word can function as one word category, or part of speech, in one sentence, and as another word category in another sentence (see Lesson 2). For example, let's look at the word *cream*. In the sentence *I brought the cream*, *cream* is a noun. But in the sentence *That's a cream cake*, *cream* is an adjective, telling us more about the noun *cake*.

## Test yourself 16.5

In each of the sentences below, decide if the underlined words are functioning as nouns or adjectives.
Sample: That copy isn't legible.   adjective

*Lesson 16: Identifying adjectives*

*Getting started* (answers on p. 63)

1. The window ledge is too narrow for a plant.
2. That window is stuck shut.
3. This has been a chilly spring.
4. I'm enjoying this spring weather.
5. The morning hours are not my best.

*More practice* (answers on the website)

6. I drink two cups of coffee each morning.
7. In most public restaurants, it is forbidden to smoke a cigarette.
8. Cigarette smokers must go for X-ray tests regularly.
9. My nephew was looking for travel companions.
10. Foreign travel can be both exhausting and exhilarating.

## Test yourself 16.6

In each of the sentences below, decide if the underlined words are functioning as nouns, verbs, or adjectives.
Sample: That's a jail cell.   adjective

*Getting started* (answers on p. 63)

1. He goes to a day school.
2. I work during the day.
3. The defendant will shock them when they hear his response.
4. It was a terrible shock.
5. I will voice my opinion if I want to.

*More practice* (answers on the website)

6. The singer had a wonderful voice.
7. Some people call the larynx a voice box.
8. Some languages have both formal and informal terms of address.
9. I don't wish to address this question at this time.
10. Did you put my information in your address book?

## Test yourself 16.7

In each of the sentences below, identify the word category of each word in each sentence.
Sample: The instructor answered her unspoken question.
  determiner – noun – verb – determiner – adjective – noun

# UNIT 4: ADJECTIVES

*Getting started* (answers on p. 64)

1. A light rain fell.

2. Ernie's friend likes a good argument.

3. His employee received that small bonus.

4. Some big cars take premium gasoline.

5. This question deserves a serious answer.

*More practice* (answers on the website)

6. The policeman's warning scared my passengers.

7. Most guests enjoyed the lavish party.

8. Your best friend had a soda.

9. Good marriages have many joyous moments.

10. His daughter bought a stunning Italian dress.

# Answer keys: *Test yourself, Getting started* questions – Unit 4

## Test yourself 16.1

|   | Adjective | Not an adjective |
|---|---|---|
| 1. yellow | ✗ |  |
| 2. wonderful | ✗ |  |
| 3. these |  | ✗ |
| 4. quickly |  | ✗ |
| 5. unreliable | ✗ |  |

## Test yourself 16.2

1. The strange robots marched towards the city.
2. It was the last day of school.
3. We tugged at the enormous gate.
4. The billowing smoke alerted us to the fire.
5. The sudden sandstorm forced the surprised bathers to flee the beach.

## Test yourself 16.3

1. Evenings were a special time for the family.
2. The next week was a busy one in the store.
3. There's an unusual idea floating around.
4. I turned a corner in the long hall.
5. A dirty fork had fallen to the floor.

## Test yourself 16.4

1. They went off to see an old, gloomy, historic mansion in southern England.
2. She had anticipated his sudden arrival.
3. Angela ignored his annoying, persistent questions.
4. I must get rid of my decrepit, banged-up little old car.
5. We wouldn't want to cross this wide, busy street, would we?

## Test yourself 16.5

1. The window ledge is too narrow for a plant.   adjective
2. That window is stuck shut.   noun
3. This has been a chilly spring.   noun
4. I'm enjoying this spring weather.   adjective
5. The morning hours are not my best.   adjective

## Test yourself 16.6

1. He goes to a day school.   adjective
2. I work during the day.   noun

# UNIT 4: ADJECTIVES

3. The defendant will <u>shock</u> them when they hear his response.  <u>verb</u>
4. It was a terrible <u>shock</u>.  <u>noun</u>
5. I will <u>voice</u> my opinion if I want to.  <u>verb</u>

## Test yourself 16.7

1. A light rain fell.
   <u>determiner – adjective – noun – verb</u>
2. Ernie's friend likes a good argument.
   <u>determiner – noun – verb – determiner – adjective – noun</u>
3. His employee received that small bonus.
   <u>determiner – noun – verb – determiner – adjective – noun</u>
4. Some big cars take premium gasoline.
   <u>determiner – adjective – noun – verb – adjective – noun</u>
5. This question deserves a serious answer.
   <u>determiner – noun – verb – determiner – adjective – noun</u>

☞ **FOR A REVIEW EXERCISE OF THIS UNIT, SEE THE WEBSITE.**

# UNIT 5: PREPOSITIONS

## Lesson 17: Identifying prepositions

What is a preposition? The prepositions are underlined in the following sentences.
1. She made notes on the paper.
2. My office is between the post office and the laundromat.
3. I'll meet you after work.

> **Quick tip 17.1**
>
> Prepositions are words, usually small, that typically indicate information about direction, location, or time. There is only a small number of prepositions in English. Some commonly used examples are *at, from, in, on,* and *to*.

The following are common prepositions:

| | | | |
|---|---|---|---|
| about | beneath | into | throughout |
| above | beside | like | till |
| across | between | near | to |
| after | beyond | of | toward(s) |
| against | by | off | under |
| along | despite | on | until |
| among | down | onto | up |
| around | during | out | upon |
| at | for | over | with |
| before | from | since | within |
| behind | in | through | without |
| below | | | |

> **Quick tip 17.2**
>
> If you can put a word in one of the empty slots in one of the following sentences, the word is a preposition: *I walked _____ the table. It happened _____ that time.*

This tip will help you identify many, though not all, prepositions.

## Test yourself 17.1

Underline the prepositions in the sentences below. There may be more than one. Use the *Quick tips* and the list of prepositions to help you.
Sample: My friends are going with me.

# UNIT 5: PREPOSITIONS

***Getting started*** (answers on p. 68)

1. Let's go into the dining room.
2. It was the dumbest thing he did in his entire life.
3. Felice was having dinner on the patio.
4. She ran to the candy store.
5. I looked for you during the intermission.

***More practice*** (answers on the website)

6. We were flying over Europe.
7. Lenore looked beneath the rock.
8. She found the pot of gold.
9. Is it over the rainbow?
10. He appeared at the right place at the right time.

## Test yourself 17.2

Underline the prepositions with a solid line and the nouns with a squiggly line in each of the sentences below.
Sample: There's a small house near the field.

***Getting started*** (answers on p. 68)

1. A uniformed guard stood near the massive entryway.
2. She leaned out the window and waved to the large crowd.
3. The older woman from Chicago had already left.
4. She staggered into the store.
5. Carissa sat at the computer in a large room.

***More practice*** (answers on the website)

6. Are you going to the prom with Stan?
7. Mike always gives a nice present to his wife on her birthday.
8. Please don't ask how my day at the office was!
9. I couldn't open the door of my car without my key.
10. Let's meet at or near midnight.

### To enhance your understanding
Don't confuse the two types of *to*:
   4. I want to go home. (infinitive: *to* + verb)
   5. I went to Chicago. (preposition: *to* + noun)

## Test yourself 17.3

Underline the prepositions with a solid line, the verbs with a double underline, and the adjectives with a squiggly line in the sentences below.
Sample: I'll buy us a large bucket of chicken.

***Getting started*** (answers on p. 68)

1. Jean walked around the grounds of the magnificent estate.
2. His friend pounded him on the back.
3. The puppy gazed at him expectantly.
4. The loud music in that store bothered Jamie.
5. He has hot coffee before class.

*Lesson 17: Identifying prepositions*

***More practice*** (answers on the website)

6. José buys fresh bread for his family every week.
7. Do you want tickets to the new play?
8. The young bride's mother seemed happy among her friends.
9. The tireless teenager ran across the park with his new running shoes.
10. I placed some small apples near the sink.

---

### To further enhance your understanding
Take a look at the following sentences.
  6. I'm standing <u>in front of</u> my house.
  7. That man was <u>ahead of</u> her.
  8. Please get <u>out of</u> his way.

Each of these sentences contains a multiword preposition, that is, a preposition consisting of more than one word. Below is a list of common multiword prepositions, commonly called **compound** or *phrasal prepositions*.

| | |
|---|---|
| across from | inside of |
| ahead of | in spite of |
| along with | instead of |
| because of | on account of |
| by means of | on top of |
| due to | out of |
| for the sake of | over to |
| in addition to | together with |
| in front of | up to |

For more about prepositions, see Lesson 29.

# Answer keys: *Test yourself, Getting started* questions – Unit 5

### Test yourself 17.1

1. Let's go <u>into</u> the dining room.
2. It was the dumbest thing he did <u>in</u> his entire life.
3. Felice was having dinner <u>on</u> the patio.
4. She ran <u>to</u> the candy store.
5. I looked <u>for</u> you <u>during</u> the intermission.

### Test yourself 17.2

1. A uniformed guard stood near the massive entryway.
2. She leaned out the window and waved to the large crowd.
3. The older woman from Chicago had already left.
4. She staggered into the store.
5. Carissa sat at the computer in a large room.

### Test yourself 17.3

1. Jean walked around the grounds of the magnificient state.
2. His friend pounded him on the back.
3. The puppy gazed at him expectantly.
4. The loud music in that store bothered Jamie.
5. He has hot coffee before class.

☞ **FOR A REVIEW EXERCISE OF THIS UNIT, SEE THE WEBSITE.**

# UNIT 6: CONJUNCTIONS

1. I saw Mary at the store.
2. I saw Mary and John at the store.
3. I saw Mary and John and Harry at the store.
4. I saw Mary and John and Harry and Melissa at the store.
5. I saw Mary and John and Harry and Melissa and ten other people at the store.
6. I saw ...

Well, you get the idea.

What are conjunctions? Conjunctions are connectors. They are words, such as and, that join words, phrases and sentences together. Some other conjunctions are underlined in the sentences below.

7. He didn't respond much, just occasionally said "yes" or "no."
8. They take life seriously but are still fun to be around.
9. I thought that he was crazy.
10. Adam left the room before Tabitha could say another thing.
11. Just turn right when you get to the corner.

There are different kinds of conjunctions. We'll look at coordinating conjunctions first.

# Lesson 18: Coordinating conjunctions

Coordinating conjunctions connect any two units that are the same type. For example, they can connect two sentences, two nouns, two verbs, two determiners, two prepositions, or two adjectives.

> **Quick tip 18.1**
>
> There are three common coordinating conjunctions in English. They are: *and, or,* and *but.* Four less common ones are *for, so, yet,* and *nor.*

> **Quick tip 18.2**
>
> A commonly used way to remember the coordinating conjunctions is to think of FANBOYS: F (*for*), A (*and*), N (*nor*), B (*but*), O (*or*), Y (*yet*), S (*so*).

But given that *and, or,* and *but* are the most common, you'll be in good shape if you just remember those.

The coordinating conjunctions in the sentences below are underlined.

1. **You asked my friend,** and **then the other two came as well.**
2. **I go** or **he goes.**
3. **It wasn't dark** but **the moon was out.**

In these sentences, you can see that the coordinating conjunction has a complete sentence on either side of it. (The sentences on either side are in bold.) Thus, the conjunction in these examples is connecting two sentences.

In the next group of sentences, you can see that the coordinating conjunction has a noun on either side of it. Thus, the conjunction is joining two nouns. The nouns are in bold.

4. The children had **milk** and **cookies**.
5. People study **medicine** or **dentistry** when they enroll at that institution.

In the next sentences, the coordinating conjunction is joining two adjectives. The adjectives are in bold.

6. That restaurant is known for **healthy** and **nutritious** food.
7. I'm buying either the **striped** or **paisley** wallpaper.

## Test yourself 18.1

Underline the coordinating conjunction in each sentence below. Remember that the coordinating conjunctions are: *and, or, but, for, so, yet, nor.*

Sample: The old carpet was worn out but the furniture looked relatively new.

*Lesson 18: Coordinating conjunctions*

*Getting started* (answers on p. 79)

1. You can hide between trips and make believe you're innocent.
2. Was it near here or over there?
3. Roger looked around but he didn't see anything.
4. They'll eat chicken or turkey for dinner.
5. Mr. Joseph pulled out three letters and handed one to each of the men.

*More practice* (answers on the website)

6. He wants to work through the night but I don't.
7. The general sent the dispatch to the army and the navy.
8. He went to the cloister or to the small chapel nearby.
9. Maud is not hungry, nor is her sister thirsty.
10. He'll come over or he'll call.

## Test yourself 18.2

Underline the coordinating conjunction in each sentence below. Then decide if the conjunction is joining two sentences or two nouns. In this exercise, if there is not a complete sentence on either side of the conjunction, it is joining two nouns.
Sample: Mary decided to have either soup or salad.   nouns

*Getting started* (answers on p. 79)

1. Mr. Eagle was called away on business, so Mrs. Broxton took his place at the meeting. ..................
2. He'd heard of it, but he didn't like the idea. ..................
3. Erin felt real excitement and enthusiasm. ..................
4. It was raining hard, yet we went to the ball game. ..................
5. The airline attendant asked, "Would you like coffee or tea?" ..................

*More practice* (answers on the website)

6. The color TV was too expensive, so Nancy didn't buy it. ..................
7. Do you swear to tell the truth, nothing but the truth? ..................
8. At one time my favorite band was *Katrina and the Waves*. ..................
9. Sammy wanted to go skydiving, but his parents didn't let him. ..................
10. For me, going to Paris is always a treat, for I love its architecture. ..................

## Test yourself 18.3

Underline the coordinating conjunction in each sentence below. Then decide if the conjunction is joining two verbs, two adjectives, or two prepositions.
Sample: That is a difficult but worthwhile lesson.   adjectives

*Getting started* (answers on p. 79)

1. I'll be near or between the stacks.
2. He came up with a quick and effective remedy.
3. I hope you won't worry or brood too much about it.
4. This trip will be expensive but worthwhile.
5. I am at or near a breakthrough.

# UNIT 6: CONJUNCTIONS

*More practice* (answers on the website)

6. Don't you hate to eat and run? ..................................
7. What size shirt are you looking for: small or large? ..................................
8. They came and went in a hurry. ..................................
9. At seven in the morning Tamara is sluggish yet efficient. ..................................
10. It is not advisable to drink and drive at the same time. ..................................

## Test yourself 18.4

Write down the seven coordinating conjunctions. (Remember FANBOYS.) Answers on p. 79.

1. ..........................    5. ..........................
2. ..........................    6. ..........................
3. ..........................    7. ..........................
4. ..........................

# Lesson 19: Subordinating conjunctions

Another kind of conjunction is called a subordinating conjunction. Here are some examples of sentences with subordinating conjunctions. The subordinating conjunctions are underlined.
1. She continued arguing <u>until</u> everyone finally agreed with her.
2. They live down south <u>when</u> the weather gets cold.
3. Jack will buy a house <u>once</u> he gets a job.
4. She listened to his comments politely, <u>even though</u> they sounded silly.
5. They stopped talking <u>when</u> it was Eleanor's turn.

Subordinating conjunctions connect sentences; however, the two parts that are connected are not of equal value in terms of the meaning of the whole sentence. There is a main sentence with a subpart; the subordinating conjunction connects the subpart to the main sentence. Here are sentences 1 through 5 again, but this time with the main sentences in bold.
6. **She continued arguing** <u>until</u> everyone finally agreed with her.
7. **They live down south** <u>when</u> the weather gets cold.
8. **Jack will buy a house** <u>once</u> he gets a job.
9. **She listened to his comments politely**, <u>even though</u> they sounded silly.
10. **They stopped talking** <u>when</u> it was Eleanor's turn.

> **Quick tip 19.1**
>
> Subordinating conjunctions connect a sentence with another sentence, which is a subpart of it. The subpart sentence is called a **dependent clause** (or **subordinate clause**). In the following sentence, the subordinating conjunction is underlined and the dependent clause is in italics: Nick decided to try to escape, <u>*although he knew his chances were slim*</u>.

The common subordinating conjunctions are listed below.

| after | even though | than | whenever |
| although | how | that | where |
| as | if | though | wherever |
| as if | in order that | till | whether |
| as though | once | unless | which |
| because | rather than | until | while |
| before | since | what | who |
| even if | so (that) | when | why |

You can see that sometimes a subordinating conjunction consists of more than one word.

## Test yourself 19.1

Underline the subordinating conjunctions in the sentences below. Use the list above to help you.

# UNIT 6: CONJUNCTIONS

Sample: She was so tired <u>that</u> she didn't bother brushing her teeth.

***Getting started*** (answers on p. 79)
1. I'll leave the note here because I'm in a hurry.
2. Nick had coached him thoroughly, even though they hadn't had much time.
3. He could see the faint glow of a pipe that Dr. Walters had lit.
4. You should stay here since they obviously need you.
5. She hasn't called here although she'd said she would.

***More practice*** (answers on the website)
6. Jake would be free once he reached the fence.
7. You were behaving as if you were the boss.
8. They were determined to go for a walk, unless it was going to rain.
9. Kevin should think twice before he speaks.
10. I am going to finish this job even if it takes hours.

Here are the same sentences we saw earlier, but this time with the dependent clauses in italics; the subordinating conjunctions are still underlined.
11. She continued arguing <u>until</u> *everyone finally agreed with her.*
12. They live down south <u>when</u> *the weather gets cold.*
13. Jack will buy a house <u>once</u> *he gets a job.*
14. She listened to his comments politely, <u>even though</u> *they sounded silly.*
15. They stopped talking <u>when</u> *it was Eleanor's turn.*

Notice that the subordinating conjunction is always the first word of the dependent clause.

> **Quick tip 19.2**
>
> The subordinating conjunction is always the first word of the dependent clause.

In all of the examples we've looked at so far, the dependent clause has come after the main sentence. But sometimes the dependent clause comes before the main sentence. In the following examples, the subordinating conjunctions are underlined, and the main sentences are in bold:
16. <u>If</u> he knew the truth, **her father would throw the doll away.**
17. <u>When</u> I brought my first paycheck home, **I wanted to frame it.**
18. <u>Once</u> he gets a job, **Jack will buy a house.**
19. <u>When</u> it was Eleanor's turn, **they stopped talking.**

Notice that sentences 18 and 19 are the same as sentences 13 and 15, except that in sentences 18 and 19 the subordinating conjunction and the rest of the dependent clause come before the main sentence rather than after it.

## Test yourself 19.2

Underline the subordinating conjunction in each of the sentences below. In each of these sentences, the dependent clause comes before the main sentence.

Sample: <u>Although</u> he was not happily married, he remained faithful to his wife.

*Lesson 19: Subordinating conjunctions*

*Getting started* (answers on p. 80)

1. Even though he calmed down, he did not go back to the table immediately.
2. While I enjoy being in the yard, I hate mowing the lawn.
3. Unless there's a heavy downpour, I'm going on that trip.
4. Why anyone would swim in ice cold water, I just don't understand.
5. Whether you are right or wrong, I will support you.

*More practice* (answers on the website)

6. Wherever we travel, we always have fun together.
7. As I was looking for my keys, I noticed a package in front of the door.
8. Just after they crossed the river, the drawbridge opened up.
9. Before anyone could shout a warning, the tree fell.
10. Since you think you are so smart, tell me the capital of Ghana!

## Test yourself 19.3

Underline the subordinating conjunction in each of the sentences below. In some of them, the dependent clause will be after the main sentence; in others, it will come before the main sentence. Again, use the list of subordinating conjunctions to help you.
Sample: Even if you get angry, I will still be there for you.

*Getting started* (answers on p. 80)

1. Sally spent a lot of time with the babysitter, because her mother had to work.
2. Since you're always busy, I decided to go to the movies without you.
3. After he read the article, he decided not to argue any further.
4. We will move to Seattle, unless you can convince me not to.
5. As if speaking Igbo wasn't enough, this professor speaks Yoruba as well.

*More practice* (answers on the website)

6. I always get anxious when I am in the doctor's office.
7. Though Tatiana passed the bar exam, she won't be practicing law until next year.
8. Did you ever wonder how children learn language?
9. Once he finishes college, he will look for a job.
10. I took the express train so that I could arrive on time.

## Test yourself 19.4 – Grand finale

In each of the sentences below, underline the coordinating or subordinating conjunction. Also, write C if it's a coordinating conjunction and S if it's a subordinating conjunction.
Sample: I work at the mall when I'm home for the holidays. (S)

*Getting started* (answers on p. 80)

1. I'm the owner and editor of the local newspaper.
2. Before Megan helped him, George would have to prove his loyalty.
3. There's more than one career that he's interested in.
4. They painted her house while she was at work.
5. I arrived early but I still wasn't the first in line.

75

# UNIT 6: CONJUNCTIONS

*More practice* (answers on the website)

6. If you can understand this, you are a genius!
7. Because you are a dear friend, I will share this with you.
8. Some people are aggressive yet polite.
9. Her administrative assistant will work on that project until it is completed.
10. I rely on Joe to fix my computer, for he is an electronics expert.

---

### To enhance your understanding
Don't confuse conjunctions with prepositions. Some words may function as either:
- 20a. I've been working hard, for I hope to be promoted. (Coordinating conjunction: connects two sentences.)
- 20b. I've been working hard for IBM. (Preposition: introduces a noun.)
- 21a. John left before they served dinner. (Subordinating conjunction: connects two sentences.)
- 21b. John left before dinner. (Preposition: introduces a noun.)

# Lesson 20: Correlative conjunctions

1. Both the windows and the doors need to be replaced.
2. Either I cook or we order take-out.
3. Neither the French nor the British were willing to surrender.
4. If that's a problem, then let me know.

You can see that the underlined conjunctions in these sentences come in pairs, for example *both/and*. The two parts "go together" in these sentences, even though they're not next to each other. These conjunction pairs are called correlative conjunctions.

> **Quick tip 20.1**
>
> Correlative conjunctions are two-part conjunctions. Common correlative conjunctions are: *both/and, either/or, if/then, neither/nor*.

## Test yourself 20.1

Underline the correlative conjunctions in the sentences below. Don't forget to underline both parts.
Sample: Either the Democratic or the Republican candidate will win.

***Getting started*** (answers on p. 80)

1. Neither you nor your friends are likely to win that raffle.
2. Both Laurette and Denise have been working towards that goal.
3. If my neighbor decides to plant bushes there, then I'll do some landscaping on my side of the fence as well.
4. Neither Don's comments nor his actions surprised me.
5. This athlete is likely to win either a gold or a silver medal.

***More practice*** (answers on the website)

6. If the train runs on Sunday, then I won't drive.
7. Both the director and the playwright attended the rehearsal.
8. Neither Iowa nor Tennessee lies on the shore of the Atlantic Ocean.
9. If they're as nice as they seem, then we'll all get along well.
10. You must call either heads or tails.

## Test yourself 20.2 – Grand finale

In each of the sentences below, underline the coordinating, subordinating, or correlative conjunction. Also, write C if it's a coordinating conjunction, S if it's a subordinating conjunction, and CORR if it's a correlative conjunction.
Sample: 1. Neither the brown nor the black shoes look good with that outfit.   (CORR)

# UNIT 6: CONJUNCTIONS

***Getting started*** (answers on p. 80)

1. They were pleased with the plan and happy about the decision.
2. I'll see you when you get here.
3. They're worried because she hasn't been feeling well lately.
4. Our encounter was short but sweet.
5. If you tell the truth, then I won't get upset.

***More practice*** (answers on the website)

6. I will be on this case till it is resolved.
7. Once she settles down in her apartment, Jane does not plan to move for a while.
8. You and I make a good team.
9. Either you or I will get to the bottom of this.
10. They dressed as though they were members of the aristocracy.

# Answer keys: *Test yourself, Getting started* questions – Unit 6

### Test yourself 18.1
1. You can hide between trips <u>and</u> make believe you're innocent.
2. Was it near here <u>or</u> over there?
3. Roger looked around <u>but</u> he didn't see anything.
4. They'll eat chicken <u>or</u> turkey for dinner.
5. Mr. Joseph pulled out three letters <u>and</u> handed one to each of the men.

### Test yourself 18.2
1. Mr. Eagle was called away on business, <u>so</u> Mrs. Broxton took his place at the meeting.   sentences
2. He'd heard of it, <u>but</u> he didn't like the idea.   sentences
3. Erin felt real excitement <u>and</u> enthusiasm.   nouns
4. It was raining hard, <u>yet</u> we went to the ball game.   sentences
5. The airline attendant asked, "Would you like coffee <u>or</u> tea?"   nouns

### Test yourself 18.3
1. I'll be near <u>or</u> between the stacks.   prepositions
2. He came up with a quick <u>and</u> effective remedy.   adjectives
3. I hope you won't worry <u>or</u> brood too much about it.   verbs
4. This trip will be expensive <u>but</u> worthwhile.   adjectives
5. I am at <u>or</u> near a breakthrough.   prepositions

### Test yourself 18.4
1. For
2. And
3. Nor
4. But
5. Or
6. Yet
7. So

### Test yourself 19.1
1. I'll leave the note here <u>because</u> I'm in a hurry.
2. Nick had coached him thoroughly, <u>even though</u> they hadn't had much time.
3. He could see the faint glow of a pipe <u>that</u> Dr. Walters had lit.
4. You should stay here <u>since</u> they obviously need you.
5. She hasn't called here <u>although</u> she'd said she would.

# UNIT 6: CONJUNCTIONS

## Test yourself 19.2

1. <u>Even though</u> he calmed down, he did not go back to the table immediately.
2. <u>While</u> I enjoy being in the yard, I hate mowing the lawn.
3. <u>Unless</u> there's a heavy downpour, I'm going on that trip.
4. <u>Why</u> anyone would swim in ice cold water, I just don't understand.
5. <u>Whether</u> you are right or wrong, I will support you.

## Test yourself 19.3

1. Sally spent a lot of time with the babysitter, <u>because</u> her mother had to work.
2. <u>Since</u> you're always busy, I decided to go to the movies without you.
3. <u>After</u> he read the article, he decided not to argue any further.
4. We will move to Seattle, <u>unless</u> you can convince me not to.
5. <u>As if</u> speaking Igbo wasn't enough, this professor speaks Yoruba as well.

## Test yourself 19.4

1. I'm the owner <u>and</u> editor of the local newspaper. (C)
2. <u>Before</u> Megan helped him, George would have to prove his loyalty. (S)
3. There's more than one career <u>that</u> he's interested in. (S)
4. They painted her house <u>while</u> she was at work. (S)
5. I arrived early <u>but</u> I still wasn't the first in line. (C)

## Test yourself 20.1

1. <u>Neither</u> you <u>nor</u> your friends are likely to win that raffle.
2. <u>Both</u> Laurette <u>and</u> Denise have been working towards that goal.
3. <u>If</u> my neighbor decides to plant bushes there, <u>then</u> I'll do some landscaping on my side of the fence as well.
4. <u>Neither</u> Don's comments <u>nor</u> his actions surprised me.
5. This athlete is likely to win <u>either</u> a gold <u>or</u> a silver medal.

## Test yourself 20.2

1. They were pleased with the plan <u>and</u> happy about the decision. (C)
2. I'll see you <u>when</u> you get here. (S)
3. They're worried <u>because</u> she hasn't been feeling well lately. (S)
4. Our encounter was short <u>but</u> sweet. (C)
5. <u>If</u> you tell the truth, <u>then</u> I won't get upset. (CORR)

☞ **FOR A REVIEW EXERCISE OF THIS UNIT, SEE THE WEBSITE.**

# UNIT 7: PRONOUNS

*As Melissa entered the door of the dimly lit Cathedral, Melissa held tightly to Melissa's backpack. Suddenly, Melissa thought that Melissa saw a shadow moving. "This is scary," whispered Melissa to Melissa.*

What's strange about the sentences in the above text? What is strange is that they're missing **pronouns**, words that replace nouns in a sentence. You'll probably agree that these next sentences are a vast improvement on the first version:

*As Melissa entered the door of the dimly lit Cathedral, she held tightly to her backpack. Suddenly, she thought that she saw a shadow moving. "This is scary," whispered Melissa to herself.*

We may never find out what happens to Melissa, but replacing *Melissa* with pronouns like *she* and *her* makes her far more palatable.

As far as pronouns go, there's bad news and there's good news. The bad news is that there are a number of different kinds of pronouns. The good news is that there are only a few pronouns of each type. Look at the pronouns themselves and get a feel for the kinds of words they are. Some of the types may have long labels, but the pronouns themselves are usually short words.

# Lesson 21: Subject and object pronouns

**Subject pronouns**

Let's look at the following sentences:
> 1a. Diplomats travel extensively.
> 1b. They travel extensively.
> 2a. Professor Susan Fields chaired the meeting.
> 2b. She chaired the meeting.
> 3a. Ben plays cards every week.
> 3b. He plays cards every week.

Notice that in each sentence pair, the underlined pronoun replaces the underlined noun. The underlined noun is doing the action in the sentence and comes before the verb. This kind of noun is called the subject of the sentence and the pronoun that replaces it is called a subject pronoun.

Now let's examine these sentences:
> 4a. Biology is her favorite subject.
> 4b. It is her favorite subject.
> 5a. Bob seems happy.
> 5b. He seems happy.
> 6a. Mrs. Peters becomes agitated easily.
> 6b. She becomes agitated easily.

Notice again that in each sentence pair, the underlined pronoun replaces the underlined noun. Here, the underlined nouns come before linking verbs (see Lesson 9); although they are not performing an action, they are still considered to be subjects. Again, the pronoun that replaces the subject is a subject pronoun.

There are only seven subject pronouns; they are listed in *Quick tip* 21.1.

> **Quick tip 21.1**
>
> The subject pronouns are: *I, you, he, she, it, we, they.*

**Test yourself 21.1**

Underline the subject pronouns in the sentences below.
Sample: We wandered around town, looking for a place to have lunch.

*Getting started* (answers on p. 99)

1. I crossed the piazza and headed towards the church.
2. Unfortunately, it was closed.
3. They simply stood there, waiting for me.
4. Yesterday, she went shopping.
5. We should get together sometime.

*Lesson 21: Subject and object pronouns*

***More practice*** (answers on the website)

6. He is the grandson of an immigrant from Italy.
7. We often dream about important things.
8. You have been to their house for dinner.
9. They often have interesting discussions.
10. Last night they drove to San Francisco.

### Object pronouns

7a. Karen bought the red car.
7b. Karen bought it.
8a. The prize was given to Steve and Bill.
8b. The prize was given to them.
9a. I'm watching the baby.
9b. I'm watching her.

The underlined nouns in the sentences above are **not** subjects. Rather, they are objects: they either follow the main verb or they follow a preposition. (For more on objects, see Unit 13.) Pronouns that replace objects, like those underlined in sentences 7b, 8b, and 9b above, are called object pronouns.

There are only seven object pronouns; they are listed in *Quick tip* 21.2.

> **Quick tip 21.2**
>
> The object pronouns are: me, *you, her, him, it, us, them*.

You can see that two pronouns, *you* and *it*, are particularly hardworking: they can function as either subject or object pronouns.

## Test yourself 21.2

Underline the object pronouns in each of the sentences below. There may be more than one pronoun in a sentence.
Sample: Churchill called them to a meeting.

***Getting started*** (answers on p. 99)

1. Mary heard him.
2. The detective watched us suspiciously.
3. Stop bothering me!
4. Steven sat down between him and her.
5. Do the students understand it?

***More practice*** (answers on the website)

6. My friends have never heard of them.
7. Barry gave her a present.
8. Harry's cousin lives near them.
9. Most competitors were envious of him.
10. A strange man is standing next to you and me.

## Test yourself 21.3

Decide if each pronoun below is a subject or object pronoun.
Sample: we subject

# UNIT 7: PRONOUNS

*Getting started* (answers on p. 99)

1. them
2. he
3. I
4. us
5. her

*More practice* (answers on the website)

6. they
7. she
8. me
9. him
10. we

## Test yourself 21.4

Underline the pronouns in each of the sentences below. Identify each either as a subject pronoun or an object pronoun. Keep in mind that the pronouns *you* and *it* can be either subject or object pronouns, depending on how they are being used. There may be more than one pronoun in a sentence. Sample: You really did it right. (subject; object)

*Getting started* (answers on p. 99)

1. The clerk had been sent to work with him.
2. The research required them to work closely together.
3. It is brighter than that other lamp.
4. If you know the answer, please tell me.
5. We will be moving near you.

*More practice* (answers on the website)

6. They were hiding in the bushes.
7. I am giving it to you.
8. He went too far this time.
9. Theresa's parents worried about her.
10. She hears from him often.

---

You know that when you're talking about yourself, you use the pronouns *I* or *me*, and when you're talking about a group of people, you use the pronouns *they* or *them*. That is, we choose different pronouns depending on the person or thing the pronouns refer to. Pronouns that vary in this way are called personal pronouns. Subject and object pronouns are types of personal pronouns; see Lessons 22 and 24 for two other kinds.

Personal pronouns that refer to the speaker in a conversation, like *I* and *we*, are called first person pronouns. Those that refer to the listener, like *you*, are called second person pronouns. And those that refer to anyone or anything else, like *he* or *they*, are called third person pronouns.

In addition, pronouns that refer to only one person or thing, like *I* and *he*, are called singular pronouns; those that refer to more than one person or thing, like *we* and *they*, are called plural pronouns.

Here's a complete breakdown of the subject and object pronouns:

|   | Subject | Object |
| --- | --- | --- |
| First person singular | I | me |
| Second person singular | you | you |
| Third person singular | he, she, it | him, her, it |
| First person plural | we | us |
| Second person plural | you | you |
| Third person plural | they | them |

# Lesson 22: Reflexive pronouns

Do the following sentences seem strange to you?
1. John Smith saw John Smith in the mirror.
2. My friends were talking among my friends.
3. Sam's only cat was grooming Sam's only cat.

These sentences are strange because they're missing reflexive pronouns, those pronouns that end in -*self* or -*selves*. As you can see from the sentences below, we use reflexive pronouns whenever we refer to the same person or thing more than once in the same basic sentence. Sentences 1-3 should be stated like this:

4. John Smith saw himself in the mirror.
5. My best friends were talking among themselves.
6. Sam's only cat was grooming herself.

Here are some more examples, first without and then with a reflexive pronoun.

7a. The boy washed the boy.
7b. The boy washed himself.
8a. Tom and Harry watched Tom and Harry on the video.
8b. Tom and Harry watched themselves on the video.
9a. You can see you doing that.
9b. You can see yourself doing that.

Notice that if we hear, for example, *The boy washed the boy*, without a reflexive pronoun, then we assume that someone's talking about two different boys. Similarly, the sentence *He shaved him* suggests that the person (a male) who did the shaving and the person (a male) who received the shaving are not the same. The reflexive pronoun lets the listener know that the speaker is referring to the same person or thing.

*Quick tip* 22.1 lists the reflexive pronouns. They're easy to identify because they all end in -*self* or -*selves* (*Quick tip* 22.2).

> **Quick tip 22.1**
>
> The reflexive pronouns are: *myself, yourself, himself, herself, itself, ourselves, yourselves, themselves*.

> **Quick tip 22.2**
>
> All the reflexive pronouns end in -*self* (singular) or -*selves* (plural).

## Test yourself 22.1

Underline the reflexive pronouns in each of the sentences below.
Sample: That computer is so smart it can repair itself.

## UNIT 7: PRONOUNS

***Getting started*** (answers on p. 99)

1. John was a person who always pushed himself to the limit.
2. Watch yourself!
3. We prided ourselves on being silly.
4. The directors of that company can blame no one but themselves.
5. I see myself as a successful writer someday.

***More practice*** (answers on the website)

6. All of you should be ashamed of yourselves!
7. Rosanna treated herself to a lavish vacation.
8. I wish my car started itself in the dead of winter.
9. Would everyone in the room please identify himself?
10. You should take better care of yourself!

## Test yourself 22.2

Underline the reflexive, subject, and object pronouns in each of the sentences below. Label each as reflexive, subject, or object. Some sentences will have more than one pronoun.
Sample: Greta's perseverance benefitted both herself and the rest of the staff.   (reflexive)

***Getting started*** (answers on p. 99)

1. I have found that I can do it when the room is quiet.
2. He noticed that she often immersed herself in a book.
3. We have known her for years.
4. Some guests told us that they forced themselves to get up at 6 A.M.
5. You don't need to explain yourself to me.

***More practice*** (answers on the website)

6. Mr. Ballantine said that he appreciated us.
7. If you want to leave, please let me know.
8. Who among us wants to commit himself to another year of service?
9. Jay's wife promised herself never to do it again.
10. Reflexive pronouns are easy to identify, don't you agree?

# Lesson 23: Demonstrative pronouns

Do you remember the underlined words in the sentences below?
1. Are you sure you want this?
2. We agreed about that.
3. I'm not sure I like these.
4. Those look delicious.

In Lesson 13 we talked about the use of demonstratives before a noun, for example: *this dog, that idea, these songs, those curtains*. That is, we talked about demonstratives used as determiners. But demonstratives can also be used without a noun following them, as you can see from sentences 1–4. In these cases, because the demonstrative replaces a noun (or noun phrase), it is called a demonstrative pronoun. For example, in sentence 1, the demonstrative pronoun *this* can be replacing a noun such as *spaghetti* or *magazines*.

It's easy to remember demonstrative pronouns, because there are only four of them; they are listed in *Quick tip* 23.1.

> **Quick tip 23.1**
>
> There are only four demonstrative pronouns: *this, that, these,* and *those*.

It might help you remember the word "demonstrative" if you think of these words as "demonstrating" something, in a way, pointing to something.

## Test yourself 23.1

Underline the demonstrative pronoun in each of the sentences below.
Sample: Lenny wasn't sure he really wanted those.

*Getting started* (answers on p. 100)

1. That wasn't really Hannah's job, but I appreciate her doing it anyway.
2. Natasha really likes these.
3. He wasn't good at riddles but managed to solve those.
4. I never thought it would come to this.
5. These are very difficult times.

*More practice* (answers on the website)

6. Those were the good old days.
7. Sean thought he would never see that.
8. This is absolutely unacceptable.
9. Mrs. Wallace would rather buy these.
10. That is the funniest thing I've ever seen.

## Test yourself 23.2

Decide if each pronoun below is a subject, object, reflexive, or demonstrative pronoun.
Sample: she subject

## UNIT 7: PRONOUNS

***Getting started*** (answers on p. 100)

1. yourselves
2. those
3. me
4. we
5. itself

***More practice*** (answers on the website)

6. them
7. that
8. us
9. herself
10. these

## Test yourself 23.3

Underline the pronouns in each of the sentences below. Label each as demonstrative, subject, object, or reflexive. Some sentences will have more than one pronoun.
Sample: Did <u>you</u> spill <u>that</u> on <u>yourself</u>?   (subject; demonstrative; reflexive)

***Getting started*** (answers on p. 100)

1. We were angry at ourselves.
2. He asked us to explain this.
3. It works just as well at home.
4. They sent these to us.
5. The baseball player dusted himself off.

***More practice*** (answers on the website)

6. You should do this for yourself.
7. This reminds me of why I should respect myself.
8. That is the way they should behave themselves.
9. We excused ourselves right after dinner.
10. It could bother them.

# Lesson 24: Possessive pronouns

You won't be surprised to learn that possessive pronouns are pronouns that indicate possession, or ownership. Some possessive pronouns are underlined here:
1. Mr. Smith explained his ideas to the audience.
2. I wish I could accept their invitation.
3. That suitcase isn't mine.
4. Yours was the best essay in the class.

If you look closely, you'll notice that the possessive pronouns in sentences 1–4 fall into two groups. The ones in sentences 1 and 2 are followed by a noun: *his ideas, their invitation*. The ones in sentences 3 and 4 are not followed by a noun; rather, they stand on their own in the sentence. We'll talk about each kind separately.

The possessive pronouns in sentences 1 and 2 may look familiar to you. That's because they were described in Lesson 14, as part of our discussion of determiners. Like articles (*a, an, the*), possessive pronouns which function as determiners can occur in the slot _____ *house* (for example, *his house, our house, your house*). Since they function as determiners, you can understand why they are followed by a noun. In *Quick tip* 14.1 we called these determiner possessive pronouns and provided the full list. We repeat them here: *my, your, his, her, its, our, their*.

## Test yourself 24.1

Underline the determiner possessive pronoun in each of the sentences below. Remember: determiner possessive pronouns are followed by nouns.
Sample: Many of our ideas back then were equally absurd.

*Getting started* (answers on p. 100)

1. The woman hid her feelings well.
2. He was younger than his wife.
3. Mr. and Mrs. Bradford adored their son.
4. Thomas and Natalie were the best students in my class.
5. Your eyes look very tired.

*More practice* (answers on the website)

6. The salesman's car does not show its age.
7. We should just pack up our things and get out of here.
8. I took a look at your face and I knew immediately that you were honest.
9. My daughter is very good about brushing her teeth regularly.
10. Gamblers are secretive about their losses.

Now on to the possessive pronouns in sentences 3 and 4, the kind that can stand alone in a sentence. Here are some more examples:
5. The Greens' tent came loose in the storm but ours remained secure.
6. Yours was the first card I noticed.
7. The scientist hurried from that laboratory to mine.

## UNIT 7: PRONOUNS

These possessive pronouns replace a whole noun (actually, a whole noun phrase, but we haven't gotten to that yet; see Lesson 28). And since the word *nominal* means "noun-like," these pronouns are sometimes called **possessive pronouns with nominal function**. We will simply call them nominal possessive pronouns.

> **Quick tip 24.1**
>
> Nominal possessive pronouns replace a whole noun (or noun phrase). For example, instead of saying *That book is Sally's book* we can simply say, *That book is hers.* The nominal possessive pronouns are: *mine, yours, his, hers, its, ours, theirs.*

Notice that the pronouns *his* and *its* can function either as determiner possessive pronouns (see *Quick tip* 14.1) or as nominal possessive pronouns (see *Quick tip* 24.1).

> **To enhance your understanding**
> Don't confuse possessive pronouns with contracted pronouns:
> 8a. It's (= it is) a wonderful day. (contracted pronoun)
> 8b. Its positives outweigh its negatives. (determiner possessive pronoun)
> 9a. You're (= you are) absolutely right. (contracted pronoun)
> 9b. Your shoelaces are untied. (determiner possessive pronoun)
> 10a. They're (= they are) leaving. (contracted pronoun)
> 10b. Their leaving early was unexpected. (determiner possessive pronoun)
> As you can see, the contracted pronoun is always written with an apostrophe.

## Test yourself 24.2

Underline the nominal possessive pronoun in each of the sentences below.
Sample: Pete and Cathy are convinced the idea was theirs.

***Getting started*** (answers on p. 100)

1. The rattlesnake is his.
2. The mother needs her nourishment and the baby needs hers also.
3. Yours is the room on the left.
4. The computer on the table is mine.
5. Ours is the next house on the block.

***More practice*** (answers on the website)

6. Theirs will probably be the best dog in the show.
7. Hiring the band is not Dave's responsibility – it is yours.
8. Whatever the neighbors want to haul away is theirs for the taking.
9. Most people's experience is probably similar to hers.
10. His is not the only opinion that matters.

## Test yourself 24.3

Decide if each possessive pronoun below is a determiner or a nominal possessive pronoun.
Sample: yours nominal

## Lesson 24: Possessive pronouns

**Getting started** (answers on p. 100)

1. my
2. theirs
3. mine
4. your
5. her

**More practice** (answers on the website)

6. our
7. their
8. ours
9. hers
10. his

## Test yourself 24.4

Underline the possessive pronoun in each of the sentences below. Then indicate if it functions as a determiner or a nominal possessive pronoun.
Sample: Jack's trip was good, but not nearly as exciting as <u>theirs</u>. (determiner)

**Getting started** (answers on p. 101)

1. Listening to music might interfere with your ability to concentrate.
2. Some of the CDs are ours.
3. The prisoner was ordered to hand over his things.
4. In my opinion, you should apologize.
5. Hers is the only dissenting voice in the room.

**More practice** (answers on the website)

6. The big suitcase over there is mine.
7. Someone wants to buy our company.
8. Some day this will all be yours.
9. The suspects had their day in court.
10. The bank is going to need her signature.

## Test yourself 24.5

Decide if each pronoun below is a determiner possessive pronoun (*my, our*, etc.), nominal possessive pronoun (*mine, ours*, etc.), subject pronoun (*I, we*, etc.), object pronoun (*me, us*, etc.), reflexive pronoun (*myself, ourselves*, etc.), or demonstrative pronoun (*this, these*, etc.).
Sample: that <u>demonstrative</u>

**Getting started** (answers on p. 101)

1. their
2. them
3. yourselves
4. we
5. hers

**More practice** (answers on the website)

6. us
7. itself
8. those
9. me
10. yours

# UNIT 7: PRONOUNS

## Test yourself 24.6 – Grand finale

Underline the pronouns in each of the sentences below. Label each as determiner possessive, nominal possessive, subject, object, demonstrative, or reflexive. Some sentences will have more than one pronoun.

Sample: <u>They</u> were convinced that <u>she</u> would do a great job for <u>them</u>.   (subject; subject; object)

***Getting started*** (answers on p. 101)

1. Their employees were working during lunch.
2. He asked us for the answer.
3. It made a huge difference to her and to her friends.
4. She looked at herself in the rearview mirror of my car.
5. Some guy introduced himself and gave me his business card.

***More practice*** (answers on the website)

6. You shouldn't compare your accomplishments to theirs.
7. The candidates presented themselves and their positions to us.
8. Are all these hers or mine?
9. You should thank him for bringing that to your attention.
10. We saved this for last because of its complexity and because the opportunity presented itself to include all pronoun types in it – but the final judgment is yours!

# Lesson 25: Interrogative pronouns

What do you notice about the underlined words in the following sentences?

1. <u>Who</u> went first?
2. <u>What</u> was the man carrying?
3. <u>Which</u> did you buy?

You undoubtedly recognize them as question words. They are called interrogative pronouns; we list them in *Quick tip 25.1*.

> **Quick tip 25.1**
>
> Interrogative pronouns are question words. The interrogative pronouns are: *how, what, when, where, which, who, whom, whose, why.* Look for the question mark to help find them.

You may be wondering why these are considered to be pronouns. Like other pronouns, interrogative pronouns represent something else, often a noun. They represent missing information, information that's in the answer to a question:

4a. <u>Who</u> went first?
4b. <u>Harry</u> went first.
5a. <u>What</u> was the man carrying?
5b. The man was carrying <u>a camera</u>.
6a. <u>Which</u> did you buy?
6b. I bought <u>the red car</u>.

Since, when we ask a question, we don't yet know what the answer will be, we have no choice but to use a question word, or interrogative pronoun, to represent the information we are asking about.

> **To enhance your understanding**
> Don't confuse the following – they sound the same:
> 7a. <u>Who's</u> (= who is) there?
> 7b. <u>Whose</u> party are we going to?

## Test yourself 25.1

Underline the interrogative pronoun in each of the sentences below.
Sample: <u>Why</u> is his approach so exciting?

***Getting started*** (answers on p. 101)

1. To whom did you send the package?
2. Whose is it?
3. What can the producer do about it?
4. How can I believe you are telling the truth?
5. Where have you been?

## UNIT 7: PRONOUNS

*More practice* (answers on the website)

6. When did you come home last night?
7. Why is it so dark in this room?
8. Which do you prefer?
9. Who gave you permission to open that box?
10. From whom did you get this call?

## Test yourself 25.2

Decide if each pronoun below is an interrogative pronoun (*who, what*), demonstrative pronoun (*this, these,* etc.), object pronoun (*me, us,* etc.), or reflexive pronoun (*myself, ourselves,* etc.).
Sample: myself   reflexive

*Getting started* (answers on p. 101)

1. herself
2. which
3. who
4. those
5. him

*More practice* (answers on the website)

6. itself
7. how
8. what
9. us
10. whom

## Test yourself 25.3

Underline the interrogative, possessive, and subject pronouns in each of the sentences below. Label each as interrogative (*what, who,* etc.), determiner possessive (*my, our,* etc.), nominal possessive (*mine, ours,* etc.), or subject (*I, we,* etc.). Some sentences will have more than one pronoun. (Remember that interrogative pronouns are used in questions, so look for that question mark to help you.)
Sample: <u>What</u> are <u>you</u> looking for?   (interrogative; subject)

*Getting started* (answers on p. 101)

1. Where did your friend hide the ball?
2. Which does Jack like: coffee or tea?
3. Ours was the only entry in the contest.
4. We kept our promise.
5. Your business is yours alone.

*More practice* (answers on the website)

6. Why didn't you wash your car?
7. He thought that the brown coat was his.
8. The bicycle is mine, not hers.
9. I mailed my package to Korea.
10. When will he arrive?

*Lesson 25: Interrogative pronouns*

## Test yourself 25.4

Underline the pronouns in each of the sentences below. Don't worry about what kind of pronoun each is. Some sentences will have more than one pronoun.
Sample: What will they buy at his store?

*Getting started* (answers on p. 102)

1. You keep hurting yourself when you go skiing.
2. We should get it to them as soon as possible.
3. Who was Bill thinking of sending them to?
4. She has a great opportunity to advance herself in her company.
5. When will your great novel be finished?

*More practice* (answers on the website)

6. Our hope is that one day we will find ourselves living it up in style.
7. That will never happen under his watch.
8. Her determination gave her the impetus to improve herself.
9. Where are those new shirts you bought yourself yesterday?
10. Our ball club prides itself on its ability to win most of our games.

### To further enhance your understanding

As we discussed at the beginning of this Lesson, interrogatives function as pronouns – they replace nouns. Note, however, that some interrogatives can also function as determiners – they can precede a noun. You can see this in the examples below:

   8. Which book did you read last?
   9. Whose purse is on the table?
   10. What name did they choose for their baby?

# Lesson 26: Relative pronouns

Here are some sentences with interrogative pronouns, like the ones you've already seen in Lesson 25. The interrogative pronouns are underlined.
1. Who was laughing?
2. Whose is this?

Now look at the following sentences, which contain the same underlined words. How are these sentences different from sentences 1 and 2?
3. I like the woman who lives next door.
4. He's the engineer whose life was disrupted by a messy divorce.

You've probably noticed that, unlike sentences 1 and 2 above, sentences 3 and 4 are not questions. The same pronouns are being used, but not to ask a question. Instead, these pronouns are used in sentences 3 and 4 to replace a noun that's already mentioned earlier in the sentence. When used this way, these pronouns are called relative pronouns. They are listed in *Quick tip* 26.1

> **Quick tip 26.1**
>
> The common relative pronouns are: *that, which, who, whom, whose.* They refer back to a noun in the sentence.

## Test yourself 26.1

Underline the relative pronoun in each of the sentences below.
Sample: The prominent oil man who bought that house is not a generous man.

***Getting started*** (answers on p. 102)

1. John's is the essay that was the most well-written.
2. His wife was the woman whom he loved the most.
3. There is no one who can make me laugh more than you.
4. Danny bought a gift which appealed to him.
5. Last week I met the man whose cousin married my friend.

***More practice*** (answers on the website)

6. In general, Sharon is nice to people whom she meets.
7. I will stand on the line which is shorter.
8. The person who leaves last should turn the lights off.
9. She saw the journey which she had undertaken stretch out before her.
10. Anna leaves a good impression on employers who interview her.

Let's look at sentences 3 and 4 more closely.
3. I like the woman who lives next door.

*Lesson 26: Relative pronouns*

In this sentence, who lives next door? Answer: *the woman*. So instead of saying something like *I like the woman. The woman lives next door*, we replace the second occurrence of *the woman* with the pronoun who, giving us the sentence *I like the woman who lives next door*. In fact, the word *who* is doing two things: it's representing *the woman* and it's joining *lives next door* to the main part of the sentence.

    4. He's the engineer whose life was disrupted by a messy divorce.

In this sentence, whose life was disrupted by a messy divorce? Answer: *the engineer's*. So instead of saying something like *He's the engineer. The engineer's life was disrupted by a messy divorce*, we replace the second occurrence of *the engineer* (actually, in this case, *the engineer's*) with the pronoun *whose*, giving us the sentence *He's the engineer whose life was disrupted by a messy divorce*. Again, the word *whose* is doing two things: it's representing *the engineer* and it's joining *life was disrupted by a messy divorce* to the main part of the sentence.

In the following sentence, what broke?

    5. Sam fixed the computer that broke.

Answer: *the computer*. So instead of saying something like *Sam fixed the computer. The computer broke*, we replace the second occurrence of *the computer* with the pronoun that, giving us the sentence *Sam fixed the computer that broke*. Again, the word *that* is doing two things: it's representing *the computer* and it's joining *broke* to the main part of the sentence.

You may remember that in Lesson 19 we talked about subordinating conjunctions, which are words that connect a sentence (the main sentence) with another sentence which is a subpart of it. The relative pronouns here are doing the same thing and in fact, relative pronouns are one kind of subordinating conjunction (and appear on the list in Lesson 19).

---

**Quick tip 26.2**

Relative pronouns are a type of subordinating conjunction. A relative pronoun typically occurs soon after the noun it refers to. Example: *He liked the teacher who gave easy tests.*

---

## Test yourself 26.2

The relative pronoun is underlined in each of the sentences below. Your job is to find the noun that the relative pronoun is referring to.
Sample: I watched a few movies that were really bad. (movies)

*Getting started* (answers on p. 102)

1. They are men who are ambitious.
2. The salesman noticed the potatoes that he planted.
3. It is worth buying stocks which increase in value.
4. The guests whom we invited a week ago just arrived.
5. The flight that was supposed to leave at 5 is still delayed.

*More practice* (answers on the website)

6. The patients whose lives are in danger need those drugs.
7. The bus which has just arrived is scheduled to leave for Phoenix.
8. Rebecca noticed the tourists who were gathered around the statue.
9. The milk that Jane bought seems to be fresh.
10. The contractor whom we hired did not show up today.

# UNIT 7: PRONOUNS

## Test yourself 26.3

Underline and identify the interrogative or relative pronoun in each of the sentences below. (Remember that the interrogative pronouns will always be in a question.) In this exercise, the sentences will only have either an interrogative or a relative pronoun, but not both.
Sample: <u>Why</u> are you going? (interrogative)

***Getting started*** (answers on p. 102)

1. <u>What</u> can I do about it?
2. Adam is the person <u>whom</u> you need to talk to.
3. I fixed the clock <u>that</u> was broken.
4. The police will find the person <u>who</u> committed this crime.
5. <u>When</u> will the show start?

***More practice*** (answers on the website)

6. <u>Which</u> do you want us to choose?
7. The restaurant in <u>which</u> we ate was awful.
8. I don't care for the earrings <u>which</u> this actress is wearing.
9. Several of the boys <u>who</u> attended the party became rowdy.
10. He's happy with the solution <u>that</u> I'm proposing.

### To enhance your understanding
Notice that the word *that* has lots of uses. These are demonstrated here:
    6. I think <u>that</u> man is intriguing. (demonstrative determiner)
    7. I think <u>that</u> is the way to go. (demonstrative pronoun)
    8. I think <u>that</u> the sun will shine tomorrow. (subordinating conjunction: introducing a clause)
    9. I think the car <u>that</u> you want was sold yesterday. (relative pronoun: introducing a clause and referring back to a noun)
You can have more than one *that* within the same sentence:
    10. I think <u>that</u> that is the cat <u>that</u> belongs to you.
And that's that!

### To further enhance your understanding
There are also some less commonly used relative pronouns with the suffix *-ever*. Some examples:
    11. I'll be happy with <u>whatever</u> you decide to do.
    12. My mother always told me to marry <u>whoever</u> I wanted to.
    13. They can travel with <u>whomever</u> they choose.
  There is an important difference between the relative pronouns ending in *-ever* and those we looked at earlier and listed in *Quick tip* 26.1. As you can see in sentences 11–13, the *-ever* relative pronouns do not refer back to a noun that comes before. Rather, they represent a noun all by themselves.

# Answer keys: *Test yourself, Getting started* questions – Unit 7

### Test yourself 21.1

1. I crossed the piazza and headed towards the church.
2. Unfortunately, it was closed.
3. They simply stood there, waiting for me.
4. Yesterday, she went shopping.
5. We should get together sometime.

### Test yourself 21.2

1. Mary heard him.
2. The detectives watched us suspiciously.
3. Stop bothering me!
4. Steven sat down between him and her.
5. Do the students understand it?

### Test yourself 21.3

1. them        object
2. he          subject
3. I           subject
4. us          object
5. her         object

### Test yourself 21.4

1. The clerk had been sent to work with him.   (object)
2. The research required them to work closely together.   (object)
3. It is brighter than that other lamp.   (subject)
4. If you know the answer, please tell me.   (subject; object)
5. We will be moving near you.   (subject; object)

### Test yourself 22.1

1. John was a person who always pushed himself to the limit.
2. Watch yourself!
3. We prided ourselves on being sillly.
4. The directors of that company can blame no one but themselves.
5. I see myself as a successful writer someday.

### Test yourself 22.2

1. I have found that I can do it when the room is quiet.
   (subject; subject; object)

## UNIT 7: PRONOUNS

2. He noticed that she often immersed herself in a book.
   (subject; subject; reflexive)
3. We have known her for years. (subject; object)
4. Some guests told us that they forced themselves to get up at 6 A.M.
   (object; subject; reflexive)
5. You don't need to explain yourself to me. (subject; reflexive; object)

### Test yourself 23.1

1. That wasn't really Hannah's job, but I appreciate her doing it anyway.
2. Natasha really likes these.
3. He wasn't good at riddles but managed to solve those.
4. I never thought it would come to this.
5. These are very difficult times.

### Test yourself 23.2

1. yourselves — reflexive
2. those — demonstrative
3. me — object
4. we — subject
5. itself — reflexive

### Test yourself 23.3

1. We were angry at ourselves. (subject; reflexive)
2. He asked us to explain this. (subject; object; demonstrative)
3. It works just as well at home. (subject)
4. They sent these to us. (subject; demonstrative; object)
5. The baseball player dusted himself off. (reflexive)

### Test yourself 24.1

1. The woman hid her feelings well.
2. He was younger than his wife.
3. Mr. and Mrs. Bradford adored their son.
4. Thomas and Natalie were the best students in my class.
5. Your eyes look very tired.

### Test yourself 24.2

1. The rattlesnake is his.
2. The mother needs her nourishment and the baby needs hers also.
3. Yours is the room on the left.
4. The computer on the table is mine.
5. Ours is the next house on the block.

### Test yourself 24.3

1. my — determiner
2. theirs — nominal
3. mine — nominal
4. your — determiner
5. her — determiner

Answer keys: Unit 7

## Test yourself 24.4

1. Listening to music might interfere with your ability to concentrate. (determiner)
2. Some of those CDs are ours. (nominal)
3. The prisoner was ordered to hand over his things. (determiner)
4. In my opinion, you should apologize. (determiner)
5. Hers is the only dissenting voice in the room. (nominal)

## Test yourself 24.5

1. their          determiner possessive
2. them           object
3. yourselves     reflexive
4. we             subject
5. hers nominal   possessive

## Test yourself 24.6

1. Their employees were working during lunch.
   (determiner possessive)
2. He asked us for the answer.
   (subject; object)
3. It made a huge difference to her and to her friends.
   (subject; object; determiner possessive)
4. She looked at herself in the rearview mirror of my car.
   (subject; reflexive; determiner possessive)
5. Some guy introduced himself and gave me his business card.
   (reflexive; object; determiner possessive)

## Test yourself 25.1

1. To whom did you send the package?
2. Whose is it?
3. What can the producer do about it?
4. How can I believe you are telling the truth?
5. Where have you been?

## Test yourself 25.2

1. herself    reflexive
2. which      interrogative
3. who        interrogative
4. those      demonstrative
5. him        object

## Test yourself 25.3

1. Where did your friend hide the ball? (interrogative; determiner possessive)
2. Which does Jack like: coffee or tea? (interrogative)
3. Ours was the only entry in the contest. (nominal possessive)
4. We kept our promise. (subject; determiner possessive)
5. Your business is yours alone. (determiner possessive; nominal possessive)

UNIT 7: PRONOUNS

## Test yourself 25.4

1. You keep hurting yourself when you go skiing.
2. We should get it to them as soon as possible.
3. Who was Bill thinking of sending them to?
4. She has a great opportunity to advance herself in her company.
5. When will your great novel be finished?

## Test yourself 26.1

1. John's is the essay that was the most well written.
2. His wife was the woman whom he loved the most.
3. There is no one who can make me laugh more than you.
4. Danny bought a gift which appealed to him.
5. Last week I met the man whose cousin married my friend.

## Test yourself 26.2

1. They are men who are ambitious. (men)
2. The salesman noticed the potatoes that he planted. (potatoes)
3. It is worth buying stocks which increase in value. (stocks)
4. The guests whom we invited a week ago just arrived. (guests)
5. The flight that was supposed to leave at 5 is still delayed. (flight)

## Test yourself 26.3

1. What can I do about it? (interrogative)
2. Adam is the person whom you need to talk to. (relative)
3. I fixed the clock that was broken. (relative)
4. The police will find the person who committed this crime. (relative)
5. When will the show start? (interrogative)

☞ **FOR A REVIEW EXERCISE OF THIS UNIT, SEE THE WEBSITE.**

# UNIT 8: ADVERBS

# Lesson 27: Identifying adverbs

We've saved adverbs for last because they can be a bit tricky. Adverbs do lots of different things and can be in lots of different places in a sentence. In fact, the chances are, if you don't know what else a word is, it's probably an adverb.

The adverbs are underlined in the sentences below:
1. I live <u>here</u>. (information about location)
2. My brother is arriving <u>today</u>. (information about time)
3. She dances <u>gracefully</u>. (information about manner)
4. That child is <u>very</u> sweet. (degree information about an adjective, in this case, about *sweet*)
5. She works <u>extremely efficiently</u>. (degree information about another adverb, in this case, about *efficiently*)

> **Quick tip 27.1**
>
> Adverbs generally indicate information about location, time, degree, and manner. They provide extra information about the action in a sentence, about adjectives and about other adverbs.

> **Quick tip 27.2**
>
> If you don't know what else a word is (and you've eliminated the other parts of speech), it's probably an adverb.

While unfortunately, we can't give you a simple rule that will help you identify adverbs 100 percent of the time, the tips below will help you correctly identify adverbs in many cases.

> **Quick tip 27.3**
>
> Can the word go in the following slot? *Mary slept _____.* If so, it's probably an adverb. For example, *Mary slept peacefully. Peacefully* is an adverb.

> **Quick tip 27.4**
>
> Can the word go in the following slot? *_____, I gave / will give my speech.* If so, it's probably an adverb. For example, <u>Yesterday</u>, *I gave my speech. Yesterday* is an adverb. Or: <u>Tomorrow</u>, *I will give my speech. Tomorrow* is an adverb.

103

# UNIT 8: ADVERBS

> **Quick tip 27.5**
>
> Can the word go in the following slot? *He is _____ happy.* If so, it's probably an adverb. For example, *He is very happy. Very* is an adverb.

> **Quick tip 27.6**
>
> Does the word end in the suffix *-ly*? Is it an adjective? If it ends in *-ly* and it's not an adjective, it's probably an adverb (e.g. *hopefully, happily, unusually*).

## Test yourself 27.1

Underline the adverbs in each of the sentences below.
Sample: They had deliberately been silent when they entered the room.

***Getting started*** (answers on p. 107)

1. She returned the book and quietly left.
2. I'm leaving for Europe tomorrow.
3. That horse is an unusually calm animal.
4. The train came to a stop suddenly.
5. That remark was too shocking.

***More practice*** (answers on the website)

6. Why don't you call her sometimes?
7. We were told to handle the merchandise carefully.
8. The doctor informed his patient that his prognosis was very good.
9. The Morgans are not leaving today.
10. Unexpectedly, the principal ordered everyone into the auditorium.

Many, though not all, adverbs end in -ly (*rapidly, innocently, sweetly*, etc.). However, some adjectives also end in *-ly*, for example *lovely, friendly.* It's easy to distinguish them. Just remember that the adjectives can go in the slot *the _____ boy: the lovely boy, the friendly boy.*

While adverbs can go before the adjective, for example *the extremely friendly boy* (*extremely* is an adverb), adverbs cannot occupy the slot directly before the noun. That is, one cannot say, *\*the extremely boy* or *\*the innocently boy*, so *extremely* and *innocently* are not adjectives; they must be adverbs.

Note that some nouns, for example the flower *lily*, end in *-ly* as well. And just to add a little more spice to the recipe, there are some words that can be used either as adverbs or as adjectives:

    6a. That is a pretty easy book.  (*Pretty* is similar to the word *very* here, and is an adverb of degree.)
    6b. That is a pretty child.  (*Pretty* is an adjective.)
    7a. You drive too fast.  (*Fast* tells us more about the verb *drive*, so it is an adverb.)
    7b. This actor's delivery was too fast.  (*Fast* tells us more about the noun *delivery*, so it is an adjective.)

*Lesson 27: Identifying adverbs*

## Test yourself 27.2

For each word below, decide if it is an adverb or an adjective. Use the test for adjectives to help you decide: *the _____ boy.*
Sample: rarely    adverb

*Getting started* (answers on p. 107)

1. happily
2. ugly
3. clearly
4. gently
5. manly

*More practice* (answers on the website)

6. predictably
7. nearly
8. proudly
9. barely
10. silly

## Test yourself 27.3

Decide whether the underlined word in each sentence is being used as an adjective or an adverb.

|  | Adjective | Adverb |
|---|---|---|
| Sample: He recently increased his <u>yearly</u> salary. | ✗ |  |

*Getting started* (answers on p. 107)

1. He was <u>busily</u> writing a letter when the doorbell rang.
2. That is a very <u>hilly</u> road.
3. They fell <u>hopelessly</u> in love at first sight.
4. I never realized that you have such <u>curly</u> hair.
5. The soprano gave a <u>masterly</u> performance.

*More practice* (answers on the website)

6. Mr. Sawyer is paid <u>weekly</u>.
7. She <u>undoubtedly</u> deserves top honors.
8. This lady <u>eerily</u> resembles my grandmother.
9. Janet <u>fully</u> concurs with her husband's decision.
10. Your new house is very <u>lovely</u>.

## Test yourself 27.4

Underline the adverbs with a solid line and the adjectives with a squiggly line in the sentences below.
Sample: He was clearly working on a difficult report.

*Getting started* (answers on p. 107)

1. Excitedly, the men dragged the heavy sack to the clearing.
2. I've checked on the situation very thoroughly.
3. Adam waited inside.
4. The old fellow left town yesterday.
5. Afterwards, he regretted his actions.

# UNIT 8: ADVERBS

*More practice* (answers on the website)

6. Your generous gift was completely unnecessary.
7. Let's agree on this beforehand.
8. This offer is too good to pass up.
9. I often think of you fondly.
10. The mailman left an unopened package at the door.

## Test yourself 27.5 – Grand Finale

For each sentence below, write ADV above each adverb, ADJ above each adjective, N above each noun, and V above each verb.

```
            N        V          ADV
```
Sample: The teacher looked at him coldly.

*Getting started* (answers on p. 107)

1. My roommate usually sleeps very late.
2. Yesterday, the girl accompanied her older sister to the mall.
3. He walked slowly toward the foggy station.
4. The experienced senator quickly evaded their probing questions.
5. Later, we took a leisurely walk down by the beach.

*More practice* (answers on the website)

6. The once popular guitarist appeared on TV regularly.
7. Successful brokers will surely receive sizeable commissions.
8. We recently had a wonderful time in Spain.
9. I will take a quick dip in the inviting blue waters of the ocean.
10. Obviously, you are not the same person now that you were when I first met you.

# Answer keys: *Test yourself, Getting started* questions – Unit 8

## Test yourself 27.1

1. She returned the book and <u>quietly</u> left.
2. I'm leaving for Europe <u>tomorrow</u>.
3. That horse is an <u>unusually</u> calm animal.
4. The train came to a stop <u>suddenly</u>.
5. That remark was <u>too</u> shocking.

## Test yourself 27.2

1. happily     <u>adverb</u>
2. ugly     <u>adjective</u>
3. clearly     <u>adverb</u>
4. gently     <u>adverb</u>
5. manly     <u>adjective</u>

## Test yourself 27.3

| | Adjective | Adverb |
|---|---|---|
| 1. He was <u>busily</u> writing a letter when the doorbell rang. | | x |
| 2. That is a very <u>hilly</u> road. | x | |
| 3. They fell <u>hopelessly</u> in love at first sight. | | x |
| 4. I never realized that you have such <u>curly</u> hair. | x | |
| 5. The soprano gave a <u>masterly</u> performance. | x | |

## Test yourself 27.4

1. <u>Excitedly</u>, the men dragged the <u>heavy</u> sack to the clearing.
2. I've checked on the situation <u>very thoroughly</u>.
3. Adam waited <u>inside</u>.
4. The <u>old</u> fellow left town <u>yesterday</u>.
5. <u>Afterwards</u>, he regretted his actions.

## Test yourself 27.5

1.    N      ADV      V     ADV ADJ
     My roommate usually sleeps very late.
2.    ADV      N      V      ADJ     N      N
     Yesterday, the girl accompanied her older sister to the mall.
3.    V     ADV       ADJ     N
     He walked slowly toward the foggy station.

# UNIT 8: ADVERBS

4.   ADJ   N   ADV   V   ADJ   N
The experienced senator quickly evaded their probing questions.

5. ADV   V   ADJ   N   ADV   N
Later, we took a leisurely walk down by the beach.

☞ **FOR A REVIEW EXERCISE OF THIS UNIT, SEE THE WEBSITE.**

# Review matching exercise and answer key – Part I

**Review matching exercise**

Match the underlined word or words to the appropriate term in each set. Use each term only once.

Sample: Merlin's assistant was an apprentice magician.   possessive proper noun

## Set A

| article | particle | singular noun |
|---|---|---|
| coordinating conjunction | phrasal verb | transitive verb |
| determiner possessive pronoun | preposition | |

1. Michael dipped his foot in the pool.   ............................
2. He had made his fortune overnight.   ............................
3. Don't pick up a thing!   ............................
4. Her gardener watered the lawn.   ............................
5. The authorities were investigating the possibility of an illegal smuggling ring.   ............................
6. She always figures out the answer eventually.   ............................
7. We've installed a generator but not a back-up system.   ............................
8. They need these tools for their project.   ............................

## Set B

| base form of verb | irregular plural noun | subordinating |
|---|---|---|
| correlative conjunction | linking verb | conjunction |
| demonstrative determiner | quantifier | |

1. You can visit more often.   ............................
2. The dentist took x-rays of her teeth.   ............................
3. I became better and better at Monopoly.   ............................
4. If Bob makes breakfast, it will save us a lot of time.   ............................
5. He believes that both people want to come to an agreement.   ............................
6. Neither his accountant nor his stockbroker was able to help.   ............................
7. She never got tired of watching those movies.   ............................

# UNIT 8: ADVERBS

## Answer key: Review matching exercise – Part I

### Set A

1. Michael dipped his foot in the <u>pool</u>.      <u>singular noun</u>
2. He had made <u>his</u> fortune overnight.     <u>determiner possessive pronoun</u>
3. Don't <u>pick up</u> a thing!     <u>phrasal verb</u>
4. Her gardener <u>watered</u> the lawn.     <u>transitive verb</u>
5. The authorities were investigating the possibility of <u>an</u> illegal smuggling ring.     <u>article</u>
6. She always figures <u>out</u> the answer eventually.     <u>particle</u>
7. We've installed a generator <u>but</u> not a back-up system.     <u>coordinating conjunction</u>
8. They need these tools <u>for</u> their project.     <u>preposition</u>

### Set B

1. You can <u>visit</u> more often.     <u>base form of verb</u>
2. The dentist took x-rays of her <u>teeth</u>.     <u>irregular plural noun</u>
3. I <u>became</u> better and better at Monopoly.     <u>linking verb</u>
4. <u>If</u> Bob makes breakfast, it will save us a lot of time.     <u>subordinating conjunction</u>
5. He believes that <u>both</u> people want to come to an agreement.     <u>quantifier</u>
6. <u>Neither</u> his accountant <u>nor</u> his stockbroker was able to help.     <u>correlative conjunction</u>
7. She never got tired of watching <u>those</u> movies.     <u>demonstrative determiner</u>

# PART II: KINDS OF PHRASES

Just as you know a lot about word categories without necessarily realizing that you do, you know a lot about combining words into phrases and phrases into sentences. As we talk about phrases and sentences, we'll be referring to many of the word categories you learned about in Part I, so check back there if you need to.

Let's start by taking a look at the following sentence:

1. The little boy laughed.

If you were asked to divide the sentence into two parts, what would the parts be? Speakers of English typically separate the sentence after the word *boy*:

2. The little boy + laughed.

Other groupings, like the ones below, generally seem unnatural to native speakers of English:

3. The + little boy laughed.
4. The little + boy laughed.

That is, we all sense that *the little boy* forms a unit and that *laughed* forms another unit. Units like these are called phrases.

So we can start off our discussion by suggesting that there are two parts to sentence 1. We could call them Part A and Part B, or Harry and George, but we'll use the terminology of modern linguistics and refer to them as the noun phrase and the verb phrase. The noun phrase in our sentence is *the little boy*; the verb phrase is *laughed*. Of course, there are other phrases as well. We'll look at the most common ones in the units of Part II.

# UNIT 9: NOUN PHRASES

# Lesson 28: The basic structure of noun phrases

There are all kinds of noun phrases and we can discover them by seeing some of the things we can substitute for the noun phrase, *the little boy*. The underlined portions of the sentences below are all noun phrases and any one of them can replace *the little boy* in the sentence *The little boy laughed*.
1. <u>Audiences</u> laughed.
2. <u>Younger audiences</u> laughed.
3. <u>The girl</u> laughed.
4. <u>The little girl</u> laughed.
5. <u>The cute little girl</u> laughed.
6. <u>John</u> laughed.
7. <u>They</u> laughed.

Of course, there are lots of things that <u>cannot</u> replace *the little boy*, for example:

8. \*My very quickly laughed.
9. \*Near his laughed.
10. \*Went away laughed.

You're probably not surprised to learn that *My very quickly*, *Near his*, and *Went away* are not noun phrases.

So what can be a noun phrase?

In sentences 1–6, the noun phrases all have something in common: each consists of at least a noun. (See Unit 1 to refresh your memory about nouns.)

Here are the noun phrases again, with the nouns underlined:

<u>audiences</u>
younger <u>audiences</u>
the <u>girl</u>
the little <u>girl</u>
the cute little <u>girl</u>
John

In sentence 1, *Audiences laughed*, and in sentence 6, *John laughed*, the noun phrase consists of just a noun: *audiences* in sentence 1 and *John* in sentence 6.

> **Quick tip 28.1**
>
> A noun phrase can consist of a noun alone, for example, *audiences*, *John*.

### Test yourself 28.1

Underline the noun phrase in each of the sentences below. In this exercise, the noun phrase will always consist of a noun alone. Some sentences may have more than one noun phrase.
Sample: <u>Sugar</u> is not very healthy.

## UNIT 9: NOUN PHRASES

*Getting started* (answers on p. 119)

1. Pirates were looking for treasure.
2. Furniture can be expensive.
3. Boys often want to be policemen.
4. People think money is useful.
5. Jeremy was eating rice.

*More practice* (answers on the website)

6. Sometimes juries make mistakes.
7. Jenny visited friends yesterday.
8. Oil is thicker than water.
9. Joel hates bananas.
10. Writers often like to work alone.

You can also see, in sentences 2–5, that a noun phrase can have other words in addition to just a noun. Let's see what those other words can be:

| | |
|---|---|
| younger audiences: | adjective + noun |
| the girl: | determiner + noun |
| the little girl: | determiner + adjective + noun |
| the cute little girl: | determiner + adjectives + noun |

(See Units 3 and 4 to remind yourself about determiners and adjectives.)

> **Quick tip 28.2**
>
> A noun phrase can consist of a determiner, one or more adjectives, and a noun. The determiner and adjective(s) are optional.

## Test yourself 28.2

Underline the noun phrases in each of the sentences below. In this exercise, the noun phrase will always consist of a determiner + noun; the determiner will always be an article, that is, *the*, *a*, or *an*. Some sentences may have more than one noun phrase.
Sample: A man stole the car.

*Getting started* (answers on p. 119)

1. The winner was overjoyed.
2. The crowd dispersed peacefully.
3. A minute can seem like an eternity.
4. The dentist gave the patient a toothbrush.
5. The couple forgot to tip the waiter.

*More practice* (answers on the website)

6. A Mercedes costs more than a Chevy.
7. The Andersons bought a house.
8. The children are sleeping.
9. The lake is near the village.
10. The professor paid the student a compliment.

Here are some more examples with different determiners and nouns. (You may recall from Unit 3 that the determiner always comes before the noun.) The whole noun phrase is underlined.

## Lesson 28: The basic structure of noun phrases

11. A man laughed.
12. Her friend laughed.
13. That lady laughed.
14. Many people laughed.

Notice that these noun phrases don't have to appear only at the beginning of the sentence:

15. The criminal is a man.
16. I looked at her friend.
17. Do you know that lady?
18. The clown made many people laugh.

## Test yourself 28.3

Underline the noun phrases in each of the sentences below. In this exercise, the noun phrase will always consist of a determiner (any kind) + noun. Some sentences may have more than one noun phrase.
Sample: My hat blew off in the wind.

***Getting started*** (answers on p. 119)

1. His doorman hailed a taxi.
2. As the doctor toured the ward, a group of her interns went along.
3. Your daughter looks great in this picture.
4. Some people keep their jewelry in a safe deposit box.
5. Jack's friend is an artist.

***More practice*** (answers on the website)

6. While driving in a snowstorm, Alex's car veered off the road.
7. Several spectators wanted that ballplayer thrown out of the game.
8. The train pulled into the station.
9. Most people are proud of their country.
10. Andrea's grandmother used to bake a pie in her kitchen for her grandchildren.

Here are examples of noun phrases consisting of a determiner plus an adjective plus a noun (the whole noun phrase is underlined):

19. The best fruit is grown on the west coast.
20. Our new shoes got completely soaked.
21. That old dog is my favorite one.
22. Every new task is challenging.

## Test yourself 28.4

Underline the noun phrases in each of the sentences below. In this exercise, the noun phrase will always consist of determiner + adjective + noun. Some sentences may have more than one noun phrase.
Sample: My young cousin got on that scary roller-coaster.

***Getting started*** (answers on p. 119)

1. That adorable baby was born in a rundown house in a small town.
2. The elderly woman wrote a short novel.
3. His crazy adventure began with those strange letters.
4. *Some Enchanted Evening* is a beautiful song from a classic show.
5. Jackie's famous father is a talented immigrant from a South American country.

UNIT 9: NOUN PHRASES

*More practice* (answers on the website)

6. These old cookies are stale.
7. A little attention often helps a bruised ego.
8. Each passing moment is a terrible waste.
9. Our new house sits on the outermost edge of this secluded island.
10. Many submitted manuscripts are piled up on the cluttered desk of the finicky editor.

## Test yourself 28.5

For each of the underlined noun phrases below, decide if it is: determiner + noun or determiner + adjective + noun.
Sample: He was not in a <u>reasonable mood</u>.    determiner + adjective + noun

*Getting started* (answers on p. 119)

1. <u>The pleasure</u> in his voice was real.
2. <u>That annoying customer</u> still got a good deal.
3. Count <u>your blessings</u>!
4. <u>Jonathan's jacket</u> is brand new.
5. He plays with <u>his new gadget</u> every day.

*More practice* (answers on the website)

6. His divorce received <u>much publicity</u>.
7. I want <u>the latest model</u> for my office.
8. Let's hope <u>this terrible weather</u> changes soon.
9. I don't care for <u>her new attitude</u>.
10. <u>The motorcade</u> passed by quickly.

Here are some examples where the noun phrase consists of a determiner, more than one adjective, and a noun (the whole noun phrase is underlined):
23. <u>The dull brown liquid</u> spilled onto <u>his priceless antique carpet</u>.
24. <u>Elderly, infirm individuals</u> really need that important health benefit.
25. <u>A worn checkered apron</u> hung by <u>the sagging, unpainted kitchen door</u>.

## Test yourself 28.6

Underline the noun phrases in each of the sentences below. In this exercise, the noun phrase will always consist of determiner + adjective(s) + noun. Some sentences may have more than one noun phrase.
Sample: <u>The pushy, aggressive salesman</u> at <u>the automobile dealership</u> was not helpful.

*Getting started* (answers on p. 119)

1. The small white dog ran away.
2. The close friends loved watching the old, classic movies.
3. Some Japanese cars are rated very highly.
4. My lovely niece arrived in a brand new convertible.
5. Those pesky flies ruined my Australian vacation.

Lesson 28: The basic structure of noun phrases

***More practice*** (answers on the website)

6. Your beautiful shiny hair is enviable.
7. The crazy idea of your nutty sister turned out to be not so crazy after all.
8. The Siamese cat was extremely sociable.
9. My reliable old friend made a terrible mistake.
10. This poor, hungry man is craving a hearty hot meat sandwich.

---

Don't forget that a noun phrase doesn't have to have a determiner. Here are some examples in which the noun phrases (underlined) consist only of adjective(s) and a noun:
26. <u>Cold drinks</u> are delicious.
27. <u>Talented, creative actors</u> don't always become <u>big stars</u>.
28. <u>Individual rights</u> are important to preserve.

Proper nouns generally don't have adjectives or determiners in front of them. *creative Nicole*, for example, is ungrammatical.

Sentence 7, *They laughed*, is yet another kind of noun phrase. In this case, the noun phrase consists of just a pronoun, *they*. (See Unit 7 to remind yourself about pronouns.)

> **Quick tip 28.3**
>
> A noun phrase can consist of just a pronoun, for example *he* or *them*.

Notice that you can have a determiner before a noun, for example, *the monkey*, but you'd never put one before a pronoun: **the he*, for example, is ungrammatical. We also do not usually put an adjective before a pronoun: **pretty she*, for example, is ungrammatical.

## Test yourself 28.7

Underline the noun phrase in each of the sentences below. In this exercise, the noun phrase will always consist of a pronoun. Some sentences may have more than one noun phrase.
Sample: <u>You</u> are always good to <u>her</u>.

***Getting started*** (answers on p. 120)

1. He ran away.
2. I love watching them.
3. They were extremely sociable.
4. We want to invite you over.
5. He did it and didn't even tell us about it.

***More practice*** (answers on the website)

6. It made me curious.
7. She left us confused.
8. I am better for it.
9. You will help me, won't you?
10. They left yesterday.

---

To sum up, the kinds of noun phrases we've discussed are listed below. While there are more kinds of noun phrases, what we've done here is to show you some basic ones.

## UNIT 9: NOUN PHRASES

| noun | (example: *water*) |
| --- | --- |
| adjective + noun | (example: *cold water*) |
| determiner + noun | (example: *a teacher*) |
| determiner + adjective(s) + noun | (example: *a smart teacher*) |
| pronoun | (example: *she*) |

## Test yourself 28.8

Identify the part of speech of each word in each of the underlined noun phrases below. It will be either: noun (alone), determiner + noun, adjective(s) + noun, determiner + adjective(s) + noun, or pronoun (alone).
Sample: He spoke in a friendly, cooperative manner.   determiner + adjectives + noun

***Getting started*** (answers on p. 120)

1. The pleasure in your voice was real.
2. I still have that infamous necklace.
3. I forgot to mention it to you.
4. Mr. Bentley is a successful businessman.
5. Cobras are dangerous snakes.

***More practice*** (answers on the website)

6. Don't forget to buy a low-fat turkey sandwich!
7. The coffee is too hot to drink.
8. She buys a pair of new shoes every year.
9. He took a cruise with his rich, generous uncle.
10. You may not know that whales are mammals.

## Test yourself 28.9 – Grand finale

Underline the noun phrases in the sentences below. There may be more than one in a sentence.
Sample: I am sharing the relevant information with you.

***Getting started*** (answers on p. 120)

1. Joe traveled often.
2. The blazing sun can cause damage to your skin.
3. The unlucky scientist walked back.
4. We turned and left.
5. Those calculating politicians responded evasively.

***More practice*** (answers on the website)

6. The beaches of Tahiti are high on my list of places to visit.
7. Cigarettes are not good for your health, don't you agree?
8. I think you should recommend this book to them.
9. Disneyland is a popular destination for European tourists.
10. Arnold hurried in.

# Answer keys: *Test yourself, Getting started questions* – Unit 9

### Test yourself 28.1

1. <u>Pirates</u> were looking for <u>treasure</u>.
2. <u>Furniture</u> can be expensive.
3. <u>Boys</u> often want to be <u>policemen</u>.
4. <u>People</u> think <u>money</u> is useful.
5. <u>Jeremy</u> was eating <u>rice</u>.

### Test yourself 28.2

1. <u>The winner</u> was overjoyed.
2. <u>The crowd</u> dispersed peacefully.
3. <u>A minute</u> can seem like <u>an eternity</u>.
4. <u>The dentist</u> gave <u>the patient</u> a <u>toothbrush</u>.
5. <u>The couple</u> forgot to tip <u>the waiter</u>.

### Test yourself 28.3

1. <u>His doorman</u> hailed <u>a taxi</u>.
2. As <u>the doctor</u> toured <u>the ward</u>, a group of <u>her interns</u> went along.
3. <u>Your daughter</u> looks great in <u>this picture</u>.
4. <u>Some people</u> keep <u>their jewelry</u> in <u>a safe deposit box</u>.
5. <u>Jack's friend</u> is <u>an artist</u>.

### Test yourself 28.4

1. <u>That adorable baby</u> was born in <u>a rundown house</u> in <u>a small town</u>.
2. <u>The elderly woman</u> wrote <u>a short novel</u>.
3. <u>His crazy adventure</u> began with <u>those strange letters</u>.
4. *<u>Some Enchanted Evening</u>* is a beautiful song from a classic show.
5. <u>Jackie's famous father</u> is a talented immigrant from a South American country.

### Test yourself 28.5

1. <u>The pleasure</u> in his voice was real.       determiner + noun
2. <u>That annoying customer</u> still got a good deal.   determiner + adjective + noun
3. Count <u>your blessings</u>!       determiner + noun
4. <u>Jonathan's jacket</u> is brand new.       determiner + noun
5. He plays with <u>his new gadget</u> every day.   determiner + adjective + noun

### Test yourself 28.6

1. <u>The small white dog</u> ran away.
2. <u>The close friends</u> loved watching <u>the old, classic movies</u>.

## UNIT 9: NOUN PHRASES

3. Some Japanese cars are rated very highly.
4. My lovely niece arrived in a brand new convertible.
5. Those pesky flies ruined my Australian vacation.

### Test yourself 28.7

1. He ran away.
2. I love watching them.
3. They were extremely sociable.
4. We want to invite you over.
5. He did it and didn't even tell us about it.

### Test yourself 28.8

1. The pleasure in your voice was real.      determiner + noun
2. I still have that infamous necklace.       determiner + adjective + noun
3. I forgot to mention it to you.              pronoun
4. Mr. Bentley is a successful businessman.   noun
5. Cobras are dangerous snakes.               adjective + noun

### Test yourself 28.9

1. Joe traveled often.
2. The blazing sun can cause damage to your skin.
3. The unlucky scientist walked back.
4. We turned and left.
5. Those calculating politicians responded evasively.

☞ **FOR A REVIEW EXERCISE OF THIS UNIT, SEE THE WEBSITE.**

## UNIT 10: PREPOSITIONAL PHRASES

# Lesson 29: The basic structure of prepositional phrases

What do you notice about the following sentences?
1. The toy is on the red table.
2. We live near him.
3. The cute guy walked Mary to the corner.
4. The Jones family traveled around Arizona.

Each of these sentences contains a preposition, which is underlined. Here again are the common prepositions which we listed in Lesson 17:

| about   | beneath | into    | throughout |
|---------|---------|---------|------------|
| above   | beside  | like    | till       |
| across  | between | near    | to         |
| after   | beyond  | of      | toward(s)  |
| against | by      | off     | under      |
| along   | despite | on      | until      |
| among   | down    | onto    | up         |
| around  | during  | out     | upon       |
| at      | for     | over    | with       |
| before  | from    | since   | within     |
| behind  | in      | through | without    |
| below   |         |         |            |

What follows a preposition? In sentences 1–4, the prepositions are followed by:
5. the red table (determiner + adjective + noun)
6. him (pronoun)
7. the corner (determiner + noun)
8. Arizona (proper noun)

As you may remember from Lesson 28, each of these is a kind of noun phrase. In fact, a preposition is always followed by a noun phrase, called the **object of the preposition**, and the preposition and its noun phrase form a unit which is called a prepositional phrase.

> **Quick tip 29.1**
>
> A prepositional phrase **consists of a** preposition **plus a** noun phrase, for example *in the closet*.

We don't have to list the different kinds of noun phrases in *Quick tip* 29.1, because we've already identified them in Lesson 28; we can just refer to noun phrases in general. So it's really useful to have this concept of a noun phrase, and it's a concept that you'll see come up again in other lessons.

# UNIT 10: PREPOSITIONAL PHRASES

Here are some more examples of sentences with prepositional phrases (underlined):
9. Let's carry the sofa <u>into the house</u>.
10. That makes sense <u>to us</u>.
11. There was a small lamp <u>on her dresser</u>.
12. Jeanie was living <u>in New York</u>.
13. The boss had no love <u>for his employees</u>.

You can see that each prepositional phrase consists of a preposition and a noun phrase.

## Test yourself 29.1

Underline the prepositional phrases in the sentences below. Look for the preposition that begins the prepositional phrase.
Sample: He knew a lot <u>about that subject</u>.

*Getting started* (answers on p. 125)

1. The fabric was between the boxes.
2. She always eats her lunch with a methodical thoroughness.
3. There was a temple near the hotel.
4. The gift was for a close friend.
5. The congressman is speaking to the press.

*More practice* (answers on the website)

6. My son had lunch at McDonald's.
7. She was sitting by the open window.
8. I never heard from him again.
9. The little boy was hiding under the round table.
10. She traveled without her husband.

## Test yourself 29.2

Here are the same sentences as in *Test yourself* 29.1. This time, underline the preposition with a solid line and the noun phrase with a squiggly line within each of the prepositional phrases in the sentences below.
Sample: He knew a lot <u>about</u> that subject.

*Getting started* (answers on p. 125)

1. The fabric was between the boxes.
2. She always eats her lunch with a methodical thoroughness.
3. There was a temple near the hotel.
4. The gift was for a close friend.
5. The congressman is speaking to the press.

*More practice* (answers on the website)

6. My son had lunch at McDonald's.
7. She was sitting by the open window.
8. I never heard from him again.
9. The little boy was hiding under the round table.
10. She traveled without her husband.

### To enhance your understanding

Let's compare two sentences with the word *up*:
14. I looked up your phone number.
15. I walked up the steep hill.

These sentences certainly look very similar. Each has the word *up* followed by a noun phrase. But in fact, the sentences are different. For one thing, in sentence 14, *up* can be moved to the other side of the noun phrase without changing its meaning:

## Lesson 29: The basic structure of prepositional phrases

> 16. I looked your phone number up.
>
> In sentence 15, *up* cannot be moved:
>
> 17. *I walked the steep hill up.
>
> Also, in sentence 14, *look up* is a unit; *up* feels closely connected to *look*. In fact, *look up* can be replaced by a single verb and still have more or less the same meaning, for example, *I researched your phone number*. In sentence 14, *up* is part of the verb and is called a verb particle. You may recall that we talked about these verb plus particle combinations in Lesson 11, where we said they were called phrasal verbs. In sentence 15, *up* is not connected to the verb, so it is not a particle; rather, it is a preposition.
>
> Here are some more examples of sentences with verb particles. Notice that in each of these cases, the verb plus particle can be replaced by a single verb and the particle can be moved.
>
> 18a. Her husband carried out the garbage. (Her husband removed the garbage.)
> 18b. Her husband carried the garbage out.
> 19a. The criminal covered up the crime. (The criminal hid the crime.)
> 19b. The criminal covered the crime up.
> 20a. Don't just brush off her objections. (Don't just dismiss her objections.)
> 20b. Don't just brush her objections off.
>
> In contrast, here are some more examples of sentences with prepositions. Notice that in each case, the preposition cannot be moved to the other side of its noun phrase.
>
> 21a. He looked out the door.
> 21b. *He looked the door out.
> 22a. The hiker slowly walked up the hill.
> 22a. *The hiker slowly walked the hill up.
> 23a. Take the pot off the stove.
> 23b. *Take the pot the stove off.
>
> As we discussed above, the preposition is tied to the noun phrase following it, forming a prepositional phrase.

Can a sentence contain more than one prepositional phrase? We started our discussion of prepositional phrases with the following sentences, each of which had only one prepositional phrase (underlined):

24. The toy is on the red table.
25. We live near him.
26. The cute guy walked Mary to the corner.
27. The Jones family traveled around Arizona.

We can expand these sentences, adding another propositional phrase (underlined) to each:

28. The toy is on the red table in the living room.
29. We live near him in Manhattan.
30. The cute guy from Argentina walked Mary to the corner.
31. The Jones family traveled around Arizona in a rented minivan.

In theory, there's no limit to the number of prepositional phrases that a sentence can have. Take a look at one with quite a few prepositional phrases:

32. They landed the plane in a grassy field near the park by the river in San Francisco.

In reality, however, each sentence we say has a finite length – we have to stop talking at some point!

UNIT 10: PREPOSITIONAL PHRASES

## Test yourself 29.3

Underline the prepositional phrases in the sentences below. A sentence may contain more than one prepositional phrase. Look for the preposition that begins each prepositional phrase.
Sample: She could see the light <u>of the fire</u> <u>in the darkness</u> <u>beyond her tent</u>.

***Getting started*** (answers on p. 125)

1. Andy ran <u>into the field</u> <u>across the road</u>.
2. That first winter had been spent <u>in New Hampshire</u>.
3. She told the story <u>of the night</u> she first arrived <u>at the house</u>.
4. The lady <u>in the red dress</u> bought a bottle <u>of perfume</u> <u>with her credit card</u>.
5. I met my long lost friend <u>at the airport</u>.

***More practice*** (answers on the website)

6. Sally arrived <u>in New Orleans</u> <u>around midnight</u>.
7. My uncle walked <u>into the office</u> and breathed a sigh <u>of relief</u>.
8. We went to see the levee <u>along the Mississippi River</u>.
9. I saw this big ship <u>on the Mediterranean Sea</u> disappear <u>beyond the horizon</u>.
10. <u>To some people</u>, that is one <u>of the greatest movies</u> ever made.

# Answer keys: *Test yourself, Getting started* questions – Unit 10

## Test yourself 29.1

1. The fabric was between the boxes.
2. She always eats her lunch with a methodical thoroughness.
3. There was a temple near the hotel.
4. The gift was for a close friend.
5. The congressman is speaking to the press.

## Test yourself 29.2

1. The fabric was between the boxes.
2. She always eats her lunch with a methodical thoroughness.
3. There was a temple near the hotel.
4. The gift was for a close friend.
5. The congressman is speaking to the press.

## Test yourself 29.3

1. Andy ran into the field across the road.
2. That first winter had been spent in New Hampshire.
3. She told the story of the night she first arrived at the house.
4. The lady in the red dress bought a bottle of perfume with her credit card.
5. I met my long lost friend at the airport.

☞ **FOR A REVIEW EXERCISE OF THIS UNIT, SEE THE WEBSITE.**

## UNIT 11: VERB PHRASES

# Lesson 30: The basic structure of verb phrases

Remember the sentence, *The little boy laughed*? As we talked about earlier, *The little boy* is a noun phrase (see Lesson 28) and *laughed* is a verb phrase. There are different kinds of verb phrases, and we can begin to discover them by seeing what we can substitute for the verb phrase, *laughed*, in this sentence. The underlined portions of the sentences below are all verb phrases, and any one of them can replace *laughed* in the sentence, *The little boy laughed*.

1. The little boy <u>left</u>.
2. The little boy <u>chased the ball</u>.
3. The little boy <u>chased the red ball</u>.
4. The little boy <u>chased it</u>.
5. The little boy <u>chased Henry</u>.

Of course, there are lots of things that cannot replace *laughed* in this sentence, for example:

6. *The little boy his extremely.
7. *The little boy near from.
8. *The little boy they.

You're probably not surprised to learn that *his extremely*, *near from*, and *they* are <u>not</u> verb phrases.

Have you noticed anything that all the underlined verb phrases in sentences 1–5 have in common? Each verb phrase has a verb. In fact, in sentence 1, the verb phrase has nothing in it but a verb, *left*. A verb phrase may also have other words, as you can see in sentences 2–5, but the least that every verb phrase has to have is a verb. (See Unit 2 to remind yourself about verbs.)

> **Quick tip 30.1**
>
> Every verb phrase contains a verb, for example *laughs, left*.

In sentences 1–5, the verb is the first word in the verb phrase and is its most important part.

## Test yourself 30.1

Underline the verb phrase in each of the sentences below. In this exercise, the verb phrase will consist of only a verb.
Sample: The family <u>arrived</u>.

***Getting started*** (answers on p. 135)

1. Freddy disappeared.
2. A young woman cried.
3. The soldiers wait.
4. I slept.
5. The little girl smiled.

## Lesson 30: The basic structure of verb phrases

*More practice* (answers on the website)

6. The music stopped.
7. We agree.
8. Last night the guests left.
9. Time flies.
10. A problem arose.

---

If we look at sentences 2–5, we see that a verb phrase can have more in it than just a verb. Let's start with sentence 2, *The little boy chased the ball*. The verb phrase is:

9. chased the ball   (verb + determiner + noun)

You may remember from Lesson 28 that determiner + noun is a kind of noun phrase. Thus, in this sentence, the verb phrase consists of a verb followed by one kind of noun phrase.

Let's look at the verb phrases in sentences 3–5:

10. chased the red ball   (verb + determiner + adjective + noun)
11. chased it   (verb + pronoun)
12. chased Henry   (verb + noun)

You can see that in each case, the verb phrase consists of a verb followed by a noun phrase.

> **Quick tip 30.2**
>
> A verb phrase can consist of a verb plus a noun phrase, for example *chased the ball*.

Again, we don't have to list the different kinds of noun phrases here, because we've already listed them in Lesson 28; we can just refer to noun phrases in general.

## Test yourself 30.2

Underline the verb phrase in each of the sentences below. It may help to first find the verb, which is the first word of these verb phrases. In each sentence here, the verb phrase consists of a verb + noun phrase.
Sample: We welcomed them.

*Getting started* (answers on p. 135)

1. He created a monster.
2. Frank broke the plate.
3. Sherry and I left the house.
4. The detective examined the old broken doorknob.
5. We resent those comments.

*More practice* (answers on the website)

6. I read an interesting book.
7. Their younger sister crossed the hall.
8. The Australian swimming team defeated the French.
9. The rich wife bought some insurance.
10. Courtney ordered soup.

## Test yourself 30.3

Here are the same sentences as in *Test yourself* 30.2. This time, in each sentence underline the verb with a solid line and the noun phrase within each verb phrase with a squiggly line.
Sample: We welcomed them.

## UNIT 11: VERB PHRASES

***Getting started*** (answers on p. 135)
1. He created a monster.
2. Frank broke the plate.
3. Sherry and I left the house.
4. The detective examined the old broken doorknob.
5. We resent those comments.

***More practice*** (answers on the website)
6. I read an interesting book.
7. Their younger sister crossed the hall.
8. The Australian swimming team defeated the French.
9. The rich wife bought some insurance.
10. Courtney ordered soup.

In Lesson 9, we talked about the fact that some verbs are action verbs, like *run*, *write*, and *discover*, while others are linking verbs, like *be*, *feel*, and *become*. The verb phrases we've looked at so far have all contained action verbs. Verb phrases with linking verbs are different from verb phrases with action verbs. Let's compare two sentences:

11. John saw the teacher.
12. John is the teacher.

In each sentence, the verb phrase is underlined, and each verb phrase consists of a verb + noun phrase. (*Saw* and *is* are the verbs and *the teacher* is the noun phrase.) But can you see how the verb phrases in sentences 11 and 12 differ? You've probably noticed that in sentence 11, *the teacher* is receiving the action, but in sentence 12, there is no action (after all, *is* is a linking verb, not an action verb). So while the structures of sentences 11 and 12 appear to be similar on the surface, the sentences are quite different in meaning.

The following verb phrases with linking verbs are different in structure as well as in meaning from verb phrases with action verbs:

13. John is tall.
14. My sister became anxious.

As you (hopefully!) remember from Lesson 16, *tall* and *anxious* are adjectives. So when the verb is a linking verb, it can be followed by an adjective alone. An action verb cannot be followed by just an adjective, as you can see:

15. *John saw tall.
16. *John saw upset.

> **Quick tip 30.3**
>
> A verb phrase can consist of a linking verb plus an adjective, for example *is tall*.

An adjective which follows a linking verb and is not part of a noun phrase is traditionally called a predicate adjective, as in the example *John is tall* (sentence 13). In contrast, an adjective which is part of a noun phrase is traditionally called an attributive adjective, as in the example *John has a tall sister*.

## Test yourself 30.4

Underline the verb phrase in each of the sentences below. It may help to first find the verb, which is the first word of these verb phrases. In each sentence here, the verb phrase consists of linking verb + adjective.
Sample: We are hungry.

Lesson 30: The basic structure of verb phrases

*Getting started* (answers on p. 135)

1. The argument was silly.
2. The dress felt comfortable.
3. Steven became sick.
4. The point of this exercise seems obvious.
5. The children got excited.

*More practice* (answers on the website)

6. You look happy.
7. Her voice sounds raspy.
8. She felt embarrassed.
9. The new director proved difficult.
10. Your pie tastes delicious.

## Test yourself 30.5

Here are the same sentences as in *Test yourself* 30.4. This time, within each verb phrase, underline the verb with a solid line and the adjective with a squiggly line.
Sample: We are hungry.

*Getting started* (answers on p. 135)

1. The argument was silly.
2. The dress felt comfortable.
3. Steven became sick.
4. The point of this exercise seems obvious.
5. The children got excited.

*More practice* (answers on the website)

6. You look happy.
7. Her voice sounds raspy.
8. She felt embarrassed.
9. The new director proved difficult.
10. Your pie tastes delicious.

## Test yourself 30.6

Underline the verb phrase in each of the sentences below. In some sentences, the verb will be an action verb alone or it will be followed by a noun phrase (for example, *saw the cat*). In other sentences the verb will be a linking verb and may be followed by a noun phrase or by an adjective alone (for example, *looked hungry*).
Sample: He prepared his speech.

*Getting started* (answers on p. 135)

1. Brady was a radio engineer.
2. The king sent a clear message.
3. Those flowers look gorgeous.
4. Most able-bodied adults work.
5. I recognized them.

*More practice* (answers on the website)

6. We adore your lovely little girl.
7. She grew impatient.
8. Your son grew.
9. Chuck became an electrical engineer.
10. The diners wanted more bread.

## Test yourself 30.7

Here are the same sentences as in *Test yourself* 30.6. This time, indicate if the verb phrase you've identified is: verb (alone), verb + noun phrase, or verb + adjective.
Sample: He prepared his speech.   verb + noun phrase

*Getting started* (answers on p. 136)

1. Brady was a radio engineer.   ........................
2. The king sent a clear message.   ........................

# UNIT 11: VERB PHRASES

3. Those flowers look gorgeous. ........................
4. Most able-bodied adults work. ........................
5. I recognized them. ........................

*More practice* (answers on the website)

6. We adore your lovely little girl. ........................
7. She grew impatient. ........................
8. Your son grew. ........................
9. Chuck became an electrical engineer. ........................
10. The diners wanted more bread. ........................

---

### To enhance your understanding

You may remember, from Lesson 8, that some verbs, for example *smell*, can be used as either action verbs or linking verbs. For example:

    17. That dog smells badly. (Meaning, he does a bad job of smelling things.)
    18. That dog smells bad. (Meaning, for example, he needs a bath.)

In sentence 17, *smell* is an action verb; it refers to the dog doing the action of smelling. In sentence 18, *smell* is a linking verb; it helps to tell us something about the dog but he's not actually doing anything – he's being something, namely, smelly.

When a verb is used as a linking verb, it can have an adjective, like *bad*, after it. When it's used as an action verb, it can be followed by an adverb, like *badly*, but not by an adjective. In Standard American English, *good* is used only as an adjective. So in Standard American English, it's not considered acceptable to say:

    19. You did good.

That's because *did* is an action verb, and an action verb cannot be completed with just an adjective. So why do we often hear people saying sentences like *You did good*? What's happening is that people are starting to use *good* as an adverb, not just as an adjective. Maybe in the future this usage will become more widely accepted, but right now using *good* as an adverb is not considered Standard American English. (In other words, don't say this at a job interview, although it's fine to say with friends.)

Similarly, people sometimes say, *I feel badly*, instead of *I feel bad*, even though they are using *feel* here as a linking verb, not as an action verb. They know that usually an adverb, like *badly*, follows a verb, but adverbs only directly follow action verbs, not linking verbs. (When people incorrectly overapply a rule, it's called hypercorrection.)

We can thus explain the difference between *I feel good* ("I'm OK") and *I feel well* ("I have the ability to touch effectively"): in the former sentence *feel* is a linking verb, in the latter it is an action verb.

---

In Lesson 30, we talked about prepositional phrases. Here are some sentences with their verbs in bold and their prepositional phrases underlined:

    20. The Bede family **lives** around the corner.
    21. Please **ride** to the stable.
    22. He **headed** toward the policeman.

Together, the verb plus prepositional phrase form a verb phrase.

## Lesson 30: The basic structure of verb phrases

> **Quick tip 30.4**
>
> A verb phrase can consist of a verb plus a prepositional phrase, for example *drove to the mall*.

## Test yourself 30.8

Underline the verb phrase in each of the sentences below. It may help to first find the verb, which is the first word of these verb phrases. In each sentence here, the verb phrase consists of a verb + prepositional phrase.
Sample: He frequently came to my office.

***Getting started*** (answers on p. 136)

1. The boat floated in the water.
2. Janice is from Kansas City.
3. Mrs. Miller is at the beach.
4. He looked for me.
5. The sun appeared above the horizon.

***More practice*** (answers on the website)

6. They live near each other.
7. I read between the lines.
8. He learned from his grandfather.
9. She played with her children.
10. Our plane flew over the Atlantic Ocean.

## Test yourself 30.9

Underline the verb phrase in each of the sentences below. The verb phrase will either be: verb (alone), verb + noun phrase, or verb + prepositional phrase. Look for the verb to help you get started.
Sample: This is for the whole family.

***Getting started*** (answers on p. 136)

1. Elinor rented a car.
2. The clowns never laugh with the audience.
3. The road trip ended.
4. The band played my favorite song.
5. They left at noon.

***More practice*** (answers on the website)

6. Brandy's three-month-old baby smiled.
7. Our neighbors just returned from their country home.
8. I found the missing piece.
9. We ran through the woods.
10. On holidays, the Watsons entertain.

## Test yourself 30.10

Here are the same sentences as in *Test yourself* 30.9. This time, indicate if the verb phrase you've identified is: verb (alone), verb + noun phrase, or verb + prepositional phrase.
Sample: This is for the whole family.   verb + prepositional phrase

***Getting started*** (answers on p. 136)

1. Elinor rented a car.
2. The clowns never laugh with the audience.
3. The road trip ended.
4. The band played my favorite song.
5. They left at noon.

# UNIT 11: VERB PHRASES

*More practice* (answers on the website)

6. Brandy's three-month-old baby smiled.
7. Our neighbors just returned from their country home.
8. I found the missing piece.
9. We ran through the woods.
10. On holidays, The Watsons entertain.

## Test yourself 30.11

Underline the verb phrase in each of the sentences below. The verb phrase will either be: verb + adjective or verb + prepositional phrase. Look for the verb to help you get started.
Sample: You look pretty.

*Getting started* (answers on p. 136)

1. Her mother looked under the bed.
2. Jan leaped for the shore.
3. The morning seemed peaceful.
4. The stock market fell hard.
5. She arrived with an empty suitcase.

*More practice* (answers on the website)

6. A fight arose among the players.
7. The TV host appeared annoyed.
8. The bull ran down the narrow street.
9. It rolled under the bed.
10. The show was disastrous.

Can a verb phrase have a verb followed by both a noun phrase and a prepositional phrase?
    23. He walked Mary to the corner.
    24. The dog chased the man with the umbrella.
In these sentences, the verb phrase consists of a verb followed by a noun phrase and also a prepositional phrase.

> **Quick tip 30.5**
>
> A verb phrase can consist of a verb plus a noun phrase plus a prepositional phrase, for example *drove her friend to the mall*.

Can we say the following?
    25. *He walked to the corner Mary.
    26. *The dog chased with the umbrella the man.
These sentences show us that when a verb is followed by a noun phrase and a prepositional phrase, the noun phrase always has to be before the prepositional phrase.

## Test yourself 30.12

Underline the verb phrase in each of the sentences below. In each sentence here, the verb phrase consists of a verb + noun phrase + prepositional phrase. It may help to first find the verb, which is the first word of these verb phrases.
Sample: I called my wife during intermission.

*Lesson 30: The basic structure of verb phrases*

***Getting started*** (answers on p. 136)
1. Vivian added calcium to her diet.
2. She knit that blanket from an unusual wool.
3. Her housekeeper rinsed those clothes in warm water.
4. I like my coffee without sugar.
5. Jack and Martha bought a wedding gift at Macy's.

***More practice*** (answers on the website)
6. He put the steak on the grill.
7. A nervous driver pulled her smoking Audi into the repair shop.
8. The young man bought his first computer with his father's credit card.
9. He rescued her from the boring party.
10. Alex met his wife near her office.

## Test yourself 30.13

Underline the verb phrase in each of the sentences below. The verb phrases will be either: verb (alone), verb + noun phrase, verb + adjective, verb + prepositional phrase, or verb + noun phrase + prepositional phrase.
Sample: He prepared his speech.

***Getting started*** (answers on p. 137)
1. Your sister is a talented pianist.
2. Their doctor operates at that hospital.
3. Robert threw himself into the battle.
4. The offer sounded unrealistic.
5. His mother went to the drugstore.

***More practice*** (answers on the website)
6. Yesterday we met a few of our friends.
7. Last night I studied.
8. The professor sounded eloquent.
9. We made a deal over dinner.
10. On Tuesdays Sarah paints in her studio.

## Test yourself 30.14

Here are the same sentences as in *Test yourself* 30.13. This time, indicate if the verb phrase you've identified is: verb (alone), verb + noun phrase, verb + adjective, verb + prepositional phrase, or verb + noun phrase + prepositional phrase.
Sample: He prepared his speech.   verb + noun phrase

***Getting started*** (answers on p. 137)
1. Your sister is a talented pianist.
2. Their doctor operates at that hospital.
3. Robert threw himself into the battle.
4. The offer sounded unrealistic.
5. His mother went to the drugstore.

***More practice*** (answers on the website)
6. Yesterday we met a few of our friends.
7. Last night I studied.
8. The professor sounded eloquent.
9. We made a deal over dinner.
10. On Tuesdays Sarah paints in her studio.

## UNIT 11: VERB PHRASES

To sum up, we list below the kinds of verb phrases we've discussed in this lesson:

| | |
|---|---|
| verb | (example: *laughed*) |
| verb + adjective | (example: *was happy*) |
| verb + noun phrase | (example: *left the room*) |
| verb + preposition phrase | (example: *walked to the corner*) |
| verb + noun phrase + preposition phrase | (example: *walked Rachel to the corner*) |

While there are more kinds of verb phrases, what we've done here is to show you some basic ones.

# Answer keys: *Test yourself, Getting started questions* – Unit 11

**Test yourself 30.1**

1. Freddy disappeared.
2. A young woman cried.
3. The soldiers wait.
4. I slept.
5. The little girl smiled.

**Test yourself 30.2**

1. He created a monster.
2. Frank broke the plate.
3. Sherry and I left the house.
4. The detective examined the old broken doorknob.
5. We resent those comments.

**Test yourself 30.3**

1. He created a monster.
2. Frank broke the plate.
3. Sherry and I left the house.
4. The detective examined the old broken doorknob.
5. We resent those comments.

**Test yourself 30.4**

1. The argument was silly.
2. The dress felt comfortable.
3. Steven became sick.
4. The point of this exercise seems obvious.
5. The children got excited.

**Test yourself 30.5**

1. The argument was silly.
2. The dress felt comfortable.
3. Steven became sick.
4. The point of this exercise seems obvious.
5. The children got excited.

**Test yourself 30.6**

1. Brady was a radio engineer.
2. The king sent a clear message.

## UNIT 11: VERB PHRASES

3. Those flowers <u>look gorgeous</u>.
4. Most able-bodied adults <u>work</u>.
5. I <u>recognized them</u>.

### Test yourself 30.7

1. Brady was a radio engineer.　　　verb + noun phrase
2. The king sent a clear message.　　verb + noun phrase
3. Those flowers look gorgeous.　　　verb + adjective
4. Most able-bodied adults work.　　 verb
5. I recognized them.　　　　　　　 verb + noun phrase

### Test yourself 30.8

1. The boat <u>floated in the water</u>.
2. Janice <u>is from Kansas City</u>.
3. Mrs. Miller <u>is at the beach</u>.
4. He <u>looked for me</u>.
5. The sun <u>appeared above the horizon</u>.

### Test yourself 30.9

1. Elinor <u>rented a car</u>.
2. The clowns never <u>laugh with the audience</u>.
3. The road trip <u>ended</u>.
4. The band <u>played my favorite song</u>.
5. They <u>left at noon</u>.

### Test yourself 30.10

1. Elinor <u>rented a car</u>.　　　　　　　　　　　verb + noun phrase
2. The clowns never <u>laugh with the audience</u>.　verb + prepositional phrase
3. The road trip <u>ended</u>.　　　　　　　　　　 verb
4. The band <u>played my favorite song</u>.　　　　 verb + noun phrase
5. They <u>left at noon</u>.　　　　　　　　　　　 verb + prepositional phrase

### Test yourself 30.11

1. Her mother <u>looked under the bed</u>.
2. Jan <u>leaped for the shore</u>.
3. The morning <u>seemed peaceful</u>.
4. The stock market <u>fell hard</u>.
5. She <u>arrived with an empty suitcase</u>.

### Test yourself 30.12

1. Vivian <u>added calcium to her diet</u>.
2. She <u>knit that blanket from an unusual wool</u>.
3. Her housekeeper <u>rinsed those clothes in warm water</u>.
4. I <u>like my coffee without sugar</u>.
5. Jack and Martha <u>bought a wedding gift at Macy's</u>.

## Test yourself 30.13

1. Your sister is a talented pianist.
2. Their doctor operates at that hospital.
3. Robert threw himself into the battle.
4. The offer sounded unrealistic.
5. His mother went to the drugstore.

## Test yourself 30.14

1. Your sister is a talented pianist.          verb + noun phrase
2. Their doctor operates at that hospital.     verb + prepositional phrase
3. Robert threw himself into the battle.       verb + noun phrase + prepositional phrase
4. The offer sounded unrealistic.              verb + adjective
5. His mother went to the drugstore.           verb + prepositional phrase

☞ **FOR A REVIEW EXERCISE OF THIS UNIT, SEE THE WEBSITE.**

# UNIT 12: AUXILIARY PHRASES

So far, each verb we've talked about occurs in a verb phrase. This type of verb is called a main verb. Other verbs, called helping verbs or auxiliary verbs, are found in auxiliary phrases. Auxiliary phrases are among the most satisfying to describe. That's because the English auxiliary phrase has a regular pattern, which helps to make it easy to understand. So here's some help with helping verbs.

# Lesson 31: The basic structure of auxiliary phrases

What are some sentences with helping (auxiliary) verbs? Here are a few examples, with the helping verb underlined:
1. She should study.
2. She has studied.
3. She is studying.

In these sentences, the main verb is a form of *study*, and the helping verb is helping to give us additional information that we can't get from just the main verb. (See Unit 2 to remind yourself about main verbs.)

There aren't that many helping verbs; the basic ones are listed in *Quick tip* 31.1.

> **Quick tip 31.1**
>
> The basic helping verbs of English are:
> a. can may shall will must
>    could might should would
> b. have has had
> c. am are is
>    was were
>    be been being

Now take another look at sentences 1–3, which have both a helping verb and a main verb. Which comes first? You can see that the main verb always comes after the helping verb.

> **Quick tip 31.2**
>
> If a sentence has both a main verb and a helping verb, the main verb is always last.

Does every sentence of English have a helping verb? Here are examples of sentences that do not have a helping verb. Each only has a main verb, which is underlined.
4. She studies every day.
5. She studied every day.
6. He leaves at 9 in the morning.
7. He left at 9 in the morning.

## Test yourself 31.1

Decide whether or not each sentence has a helping verb. Look for the main verb, which is underlined, and see if there's a helping verb before it.

|  | Helping verb: NO | Helping verb: YES |
|---|---|---|
| Sample: He talked about himself. | ✗ | |

## UNIT 12: AUXILIARY PHRASES

*Getting started* (answers on p. 164)

1. They were <u>arguing</u> loudly.
2. The frog had <u>jumped</u> five feet.
3. You <u>invited</u> everyone.
4. I must <u>buy</u> some milk.
5. Harry <u>lives</u> in Europe.

*More practice* (answers on the website)

6. Jogging should <u>increase</u> your stamina.
7. I have <u>worked</u> all day.
8. Sam will <u>go</u> fishing tomorrow.
9. Judy <u>left</u> for Dallas at noon.
10. Joey was <u>chasing</u> a rascal all day long.

## Test yourself 31.2

Decide whether or not each sentence has a helping verb. This time the main verbs are not underlined.

|  | *Helping verb: NO* | *Helping verb: YES* |
|---|---|---|
| Sample: Maggie was walking nearby. |  | ✗ |

*Getting started* (answers on p. 164)

1. You might write her a letter.
2. Congress voted on the bill.
3. Beth has survived that ordeal.
4. I could be an actor.
5. The Giants won the Super Bowl.

*More practice* (answers on the website)

6. You should do that.
7. She could move nearby.
8. My friend wants a two-car garage.
9. Jan must get that report done.
10. The sun rose at 5 A.M. today.

The helping verbs belong to different subgroups, as indicated in *Quick tip* 31.1. We'll take a closer look at each of the three types of helping verbs in the next few lessons.

# Lesson 32: Modals

One kind of helping verb is called a modal. A modal adds information, such as possibility, necessity, or requests, to the verb that follows. The modals are underlined in the sentences below:
1. Ellen can do the job.
2. I will worry about that later.
3. You should rest before the party.
4. Dennis might change that carpeting.

There are nine basic modals, listed below. (They were group (a) of *Quick tip* 31.1.)

> **Quick tip 32.1**
>
> One kind of helping verb is called a modal. The basic modals of English are:
>
>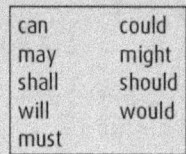

## Test yourself 32.1

Underline the modal in each of the sentences below.
Sample: William should tell you the story.

*Getting started* (answers on p. 164)

1. They must delay the invasion.
2. You will find courage in your heart.
3. Mr. Knight might go with you.
4. You should be proud of yourself.
5. Tomorrow we may go to the movies.

*More practice* (answers on the website)

6. I could dance up a storm.
7. Lauren can name that tune in 10 seconds.
8. Ashley would win that race.
9. He shall travel to the countryside this weekend.
10. Jerry must renew his passport this month.

## Test yourself 32.2

Underline the modal and put a squiggly line under the main verb in each of the sentences below.
Sample: She will be happy.

*Getting started* (answers on p. 164)

1. The curtains might hide the view.
2. Paul could work on the problem.
3. She can leave this afternoon.
4. You must go to the emergency room immediately.
5. The children will enjoy these gifts.

# UNIT 12: AUXILIARY PHRASES

*More practice* (answers on the website)

6. We should proceed with caution.
7. You may be right.
8. One would think so.
9. Mrs. Randall will give you an answer tomorrow.
10. His father can postpone his retirement until next year.

## To enhance your understanding
Here are the modals again:
- can    could
- may    might
- shall  should
- will   would
- must

Historically, those modals on the left have been considered present tense forms while those on the right have been considered past tense forms. (For more on tenses, see Lesson 37.) Note that three of the past tense forms end in the consonant *d*; think of it as a reminder of the past tense suffix *-ed*, as in the verb *stayed*.

## To further enhance your understanding
Some expressions are similar to modals but consist of more than one word. They are called phrasal modals or periphrastic modals. Here are some examples, underlined in the following sentences:

5. I am able to go.
6. I ought to go.
7. I am going to go.
8. I would like to go.
9. I have to go.
10. I need to go.

Notice that many of the phrasal modals have the same meaning as one of the one-word modals; for example:, *am able to* = *can*, *ought to* = *should*, *am going to* = *will*.

11. I am able to go = I can go.
12. I ought to go = I should go.
13. I am going to go = I will go.

Note also that phrasal verbs end in *to*, which is followed by the base form of the verb.

# Lesson 33: Perfect *have*

In each of the sentences below, the helping verb is a form of *have* – either *have*, *has*, or *had* – and is underlined. (These were listed in group (b) of *Quick tip* 31.1.)
1. She had greeted me happily.
2. They have eaten dinner early today.
3. He has written many articles about the wealthy.

Sentences with the helping verb *have* are said to be expressed in the **perfect aspect**, which adds information to the main verb about real-world time. For example, in sentence 2, using *have* indicates that the action began in the past and is complete.

> **Quick tip 33.1**
>
> One kind of helping verb is the verb *have*. It has three forms: *have*, *has*, and *had*.

## Test yourself 33.1

Underline the *have* helping verb in each of the sentences below. It may be in any of the three forms of *have*. In these sentences, it will always be directly before the main verb.
Sample: I have imagined this for years.

***Getting started*** (answers on p. 164)

1. The bridge had collapsed.
2. That cheerful woman has saved the day.
3. My uncles have visited us every summer.
4. Her neighbor has been an attorney for twenty years.
5. Suzie had traveled to Belgium twice before.

***More practice*** (answers on the website)

6. My friend Sal has bought two suits recently.
7. Your remarks have entertained me enormously.
8. Our teacher had sent us an e-mail yesterday.
9. That thought never has crossed my mind.
10. You and I have played chess numerous times.

## Test yourself 33.2

Underline the *have* helping verb and put a squiggly line under the main verb in each of the sentences below.
Sample: He had annoyed his boss.

***Getting started*** (answers on p. 165)

1. Joan and Sam have worked for hours.
2. Their mother has spoken of you often.
3. The prime minister had written to him.
4. Your daughter has grown a lot taller.
5. She has seen her friends twice since last Sunday.

# UNIT 12: AUXILIARY PHRASES

***More practice*** (answers on the website)

6. Our dogs have made a mess of the living room.
7. You had warned me not to heed his advice.
8. The chef has prepared this dish perfectly.
9. We have thought about your suggestion seriously.
10. The actors had rehearsed for about an hour.

---

The verb *have* is not used only as a helping verb in English. It can also be the main verb in a sentence. Here are some examples with *have* used as the main verb. Notice that when *have* is being used as the main verb, it refers to the notion of possession or ownership.

4. I have a comfortable bed.
5. She has a beautiful home.
6. That family had a lot of problems.

> **Quick tip 33.2**
>
> *Have* can be used as a helping verb or as a main verb. When *have* is used as the main verb, it refers to the idea of possession. When *have* is used as the helping verb, it is always followed by another verb.

## Test yourself 33.3

Decide if the forms of *have* in the following sentences are being used as helping verbs or as main verbs.

|  | Helping verb | Main verb |
|---|---|---|
| Sample: Jack had a good time. |  | x |

***Getting started*** (answers on p. 165)

1. Jack has experienced a good time.
2. He has seen her often.
3. You have a lot of DVDs.
4. She had tacos for dinner.
5. Your professor has the answer to your question.

***More practice*** (answers on the website)

6. Grandpa has slept on the couch often.
7. Aisha had trouble with her car this morning.
8. My aunt has a treadmill in her basement.
9. Mrs. Stein had called the paramedics.
10. They have donated that coat to charity.

## Lesson 33: Perfect have

You may have noticed that sometimes there are sentences with two occurrences of *have*. Here are some examples.

    7. Jack has had a bad time.
    8. The mayor had had a close election.
    9. We have had a delicious dinner.

How can we account for this? The first occurrence of *have* is a helping verb; the second occurrence of *have* is the main verb (and refers to possession). That is, just as any other main verb can use *have* as a helping verb, the main verb *have* can also use *have* as a helping verb. That results in two forms of *have* in the same sentence.

# Lesson 34: Progressive *be*

In each of the sentences below, the helping verb is a form of the verb *be* and is underlined.
1. She <u>is</u> leaving on the train.
2. I <u>was</u> thinking about his behavior.
3. They <u>were</u> managing the restaurant.

(These were listed in group (c) of *Quick tip* 31.1.) In addition to the forms *is*, *was*, and *were*, additional forms of *be* are *am*, *are*, *be*, *been*, and *being*.

Sentences with the helping verb *be* are said to be expressed in the **progressive** or **continuous aspect**, which usually indicates that the action takes place over a period of time.

> **Quick tip 34.1**
>
> One kind of helping verb is *be*. It has the following forms: *am, is, are, was, were, be, been,* and *being*.

## Test yourself 34.1

Underline the form of the *be* helping verb in each of the sentences below.
Sample: He <u>was</u> exercising regularly.

***Getting started*** (answers on p. 165)

1. The reporter was writing her story.
2. He is controlling his temper.
3. You are learning about syntax.
4. They were watching a movie last Sunday.
5. I am doing a lot of things right now.

***More practice*** (answers on the website)

6. The politicians are campaigning in full force.
7. The football teams were finishing the season.
8. Catherine is learning to speak French.
9. Those actors were rehearsing.
10. I was cleaning my closet yesterday.

## Test yourself 34.2

Underline the *be* helping verb and put a squiggly line under the main verb in each of the sentences below.
Sample: He <u>is</u> greeting his boss.

***Getting started*** (answers on p. 165)

1. I was talking to Harry.
2. Irving and Annie are studying Latin.
3. He is testing her loyalty.
4. I am taking a walk.
5. You were reading for hours.

***More practice*** (answers on the website)

6. The train is arriving.
7. The wrestlers are getting ready to compete.
8. The manager was closing the store.
9. I am organizing a luncheon for him.
10. The children were playing peacefully.

## Lesson 34: Progressive be

The verb *be* is not used only as a helping verb in English. It can also be the main verb in a sentence, in which case it's a linking verb. (This was discussed in Lesson 9.) As a reminder, here are some sentences with *be* used as the main verb:

4. I am happy
5. She was an actress.
6. Those Broadway shows are great.

> **Quick tip 34.2**
>
> *Be* and its forms can be used as a helping verb or as a main verb. When *be* is used as the helping verb, it is always followed by another verb.

### Test yourself 34.3

Decide if the forms of *be* in the following sentences are being used as helping verbs or as main verbs.

|  | Helping verb | Main verb |
|---|---|---|
| Sample: Joan is a genius. |  | ✗ |

***Getting started*** (answers on p. 165)

1. Sam is looking at the mail.
2. That concept was difficult.
3. You are helping her a lot.
4. I am a doctor.
5. They were watching TV.

***More practice*** (answers on the website)

6. She was writing her term paper.
7. David is a famous opera singer.
8. You are joking, right?
9. His employees are happy about it.
10. Jackie and Richard were friends.

---

You may have noticed that sometimes there are sentences with two occurrences of *be*. Here are some examples:

7. Andrew is being a nuisance.
8. My friends were being courageous.
9. They are being clowns.

How can we account for this? The first occurrence of *be* is a helping verb; the second occurrence of *be* is the main verb. That is, just as any other main verb can use *be* as a helping verb, the main verb *be* can also use *be* as a helping verb. That results in two forms of *be* in the same sentence.

# Lesson 35: Combining auxiliary verbs

All the sentences with helping (auxiliary) verbs that we've looked at so far have had only one helping verb. It's possible, however, for a sentence to have more than one helping verb. Here are some examples of sentences with two helping verbs; the helping verbs are underlined. (Remember that there are three kinds of helping verbs: (a) modals (e.g. *should*, *can*, *might*), (b) *have*, and (c) *be*. See Lessons 32–34.)
1. She should have studied.   (modal + *have*)
2. She may be studying.   (modal + *be*)
3. She has been studying.   (*have* + *be*)

When a sentence has two helping verbs, which helping verb is first? If a sentence has a modal, that will always be the first helping verb, as you can see in sentences 1 and 2. If a sentence has both *have* and *be* as helping verbs, *have* will always be first, as you can see in sentence 3.

Can you think of a sentence with three helping verbs? Sentences 4 and 5 have three helping verbs (underlined):
4. She should have been studying.
5. Mary might have been looking at him.

If there are three helping verbs, they are always in the following order: modal + *have* + *be*, as you can see from sentences 4 and 5. And if there are only two helping verbs, they're still in this relative order, with modal first, and *have* before *be*.

> **Quick tip 35.1**
>
> A sentence can have zero, one, or more than one helping verb. If there is more than one, they will always be in the following relative order: modal +*have* +*be*.

## Test yourself 35.1

For each sentence below, underline the main verb. Then decide if the sentence has zero, one, two, or three helping verbs before the main verb.
Sample: They may rent a car at the terminal.   1

*Getting started* (answers on p. 165)

1. She was focusing on the mirror.
2. Andy should have been enjoying his new career.
3. Mrs. Packard's life changed at that point.
4. You can have two scoops of ice cream.
5. I might have committed a serious error.

Lesson 35: Combining auxiliary verbs

*More practice* (answers on the website)

6. Tamara has been working for 22 years.
7. He could have been telling the truth.
8. The birds were chirping early in the morning.
9. Gauguin painted in Tahiti.
10. Tomorrow we will go to the movies.

## Test yourself 35.2

Underline each helping verb in the sentences below. Each sentence will have at least one helping verb.
Sample: The children <u>have been</u> working hard.

*Getting started* (answers on p. 165)

1. You should read this book.
2. She had been greeting me happily.
3. Janice might have gotten the flu.
4. My question was bothering him.
5. The prime suspect might have been telling the truth.

*More practice* (answers on the website)

6. He could have been a hero.
7. The journalists will be traveling throughout Canada.
8. I have written many articles about the wealthy.
9. This has been a difficult time for me.
10. The trial has been going on far too long.

## Test yourself 35.3

Underline each helping verb in the sentences below. A sentence will have anywhere from zero to three helping verbs.
Sample: He and Bill shook hands.   (No helping verb.)

*Getting started* (answers on p. 166)

1. I had been writing to him often.
2. Their mother has spoken of you a lot.
3. Sam will recognize it immediately.
4. We were good friends.
5. You should be studying right now.

*More practice* (answers on the website)

6. He may have been working on the project.
7. We had a sudden downpour.
8. This storm will pass soon.
9. The attorney may have overstated her case.
10. This relationship is improving rapidly.

## Test yourself 35.4

Underline each helping verb in the sentences below and put a squiggly line under the main verb. A sentence will have anywhere from zero to three helping verbs.
Sample: Paul <u>was</u> offering me a drink.

## UNIT 12: AUXILIARY PHRASES

***Getting started*** (answers on p. 166)

1. They can do the research.
2. Suzanne might be leaving sooner.
3. Papa has been teasing him.
4. I might have been being too cautious.
5. The plane was late.

***More practice*** (answers on the website)

6. The student will have completed his assignment by tomorrow.
7. You are being silly.
8. Everyone has had a great time at the party.
9. The show was a great success.
10. It must have been difficult to do that.

# Lesson 36: The suffixes of auxiliary verbs

Each helping verb is actually a two-part package. There's the helping verb itself, and then there's the effect that the helping verb has on the verb that follows it.

Look at the sentences below. In each of them, the helping verb is a form of progressive *be* (underlined). What effect does progressive *be* have on the verb that follows it?
1. The children were working hard.
2. I am considering a new job offer.
3. Nothing was limiting his development.
4. Many new advances are emerging.
5. Sam is watching his favorite TV show.

You can see that the verb after the form of *be* always has *-ing* added to its base. This *-ing* form of the verb is referred to as the present participle in traditional grammar.

> **Quick tip 36.1**
>
> When the helping verb is progressive *be*, the next verb always has *-ing* added to its base form. Example: *is sleeping*. The *-ing* verb form is called the present participle.

## Test yourself 36.1

Each of the following sentences has a form of the helping verb *be*. Underline the *be* verb and the *-ing* ending of the following verb.
Sample: Maggie is sleeping now.

***Getting started*** (answers on p. 166)

1. She is leaving on the ten o'clock train.
2. The curtains were masking the view.
3. I was wondering about his behavior.
4. Paul is leaning on his wife's chair.
5. They are sounding rather defensive.

***More practice*** (answers on the website)

6. We were attending a graduation ceremony last week.
7. Jim's parents were watching a movie.
8. You are trying too hard.
9. I am dreaming of a gentle snowfall.
10. The President was addressing the nation yesterday.

In each of the following sentences, the helping verb is a form of *have* (underlined). What effect does *have* have on the verb that follows it? (This is a little trickier than the pattern with *be*.)
6. She had greeted me happily.
7. They have eaten dinner early today.
8. That had interested the reporter.
9. Sarah had managed to pry apart the shells.

## UNIT 12: AUXILIARY PHRASES

10. Carla and Raphael <u>have</u> written many books together.
11. He and Bill <u>had</u> shaken hands.

The verb following *have* most frequently has the suffix *-en* or *-ed* added to it. The form of the verb following the helping verb *have* is traditionally called the past participle.

> **Quick tip 36.2**
>
> When *have* is the helping verb, the next verb typically has *-ed* or *-en* added to its base form. Examples: *has eaten, have watched*. The verb form following the helping verb *have* is called the past participle.

### Test yourself 36.2

Each of the following sentences has a form of the helping verb *have*. Underline the *have* and the *-ed* or *-en* ending of the following verb.
Sample: You <u>had</u> manag<u>ed</u> the situation very well.

***Getting started*** (answers on p. 166)

1. The women had spoken to each other recently.
2. Unfortunately, the heroine had married the villain.
3. Andy and George have enjoyed themselves enormously.
4. My student has written an interesting essay on technology.
5. The hockey game has ended in a tie.

***More practice*** (answers on the website)

6. The local theater has provided much entertainment over the years.
7. I have seen you somewhere before.
8. Her brother has broken the vase to pieces.
9. They have lied too many times.
10. Mona's boyfriend has surprised her with a wedding proposal.

The *-ed* and *-en* suffixes are the most common endings for past participles. However, for historical reasons, there are actually several ways to form past participles. Note the following patterns of some typical verbs:

| Verb base | Perfect | Past participle |
|---|---|---|
| be | have been | been |
| see | have seen | seen |
| give | have given | given |
| arrange | have arranged | arranged |
| walk | have walked | walked |
| play | have played | played |

Another way to form past participles is by changing a vowel of the verb base, sometimes also adding the suffix *-en*. Some examples are:

| Verb base | Perfect | Past participle |
|---|---|---|
| begin | have begun | begun |
| sing | have sung | sung |
| speak | have spoken | spoken |
| weave | have woven | woven |

## Lesson 36: The suffixes of auxiliary verbs

Sometimes no change at all is made to the verb:

| Verb base | Perfect | Past participle |
|---|---|---|
| hit | have hit | hit |
| come | have come | come |

There is no magic or hard and fast rule to determine what the past participle of a particular verb is. We simply have to memorize it when we learn English.

In each of the following sentences, the helping verb is a modal (underlined). What effect does a modal have on the verb that follows it?

12. The piano salesman <u>should</u> consider his actions.
13. He <u>will</u> recognize it immediately.
14. Sam <u>could</u> be a star quarterback.
15. The major <u>may</u> speak to you later.

> **Quick tip 36.3**
>
> When the helping verb is a modal, the next verb is always in its base form. Example: can study.

### Test yourself 36.3

Each of the following sentences has a modal helping verb. Underline the modal and put a squiggly line under the verb following it, which will be in its base form.
Sample: He <u>should</u> oppose their actions.

***Getting started*** (answers on p. 166)

1. Richard will believe the truth.
2. The waiter might bring it.
3. They may be home late.
4. We shall overcome this obstacle.
5. I would do it in an instant.

***More practice*** (answers on the website)

6. The mail should arrive by noon.
7. Michael can build anything.
8. The waiters must wash their hands often.
9. On a clear day, you could see for miles.
10. The train will make a stop in Atlanta.

What happens to the following verb if there is more than one helping verb in a sentence? Is the pattern the same when a helping verb is followed by another helping verb, rather than the main verb? The patterns we have talked about are the same, whether there is one helping verb or more than one helping verb in a sentence. You can see this in the following sentences:

16. They **have** <u>been</u> see<u>ing</u> the doctor regularly.
17. You **have been** observ<u>ing</u> the situation closely.

Since *have* (in bold) is a helping verb in these sentences, the next verb, *be*, gets the *-en* ending (also in bold). And since *be* (underlined) is also a helping verb, the verb after *be* gets the *-ing* ending (also underlined).

# UNIT 12: AUXILIARY PHRASES

We can also see consistent patterns in the following two sentences:
18. They **should** have seen the doctor regularly.
19. You **might** be observing the situation closely.

In sentence 18 the modal (in bold) causes the next verb, *have*, to be in its base form. The *have* helping verb then affects the form of the next verb, the main verb *see*, which appears in its past participle form, *seen*. Similarly, in sentence 19 the modal, *might*, causes the next verb, *be*, to be in its base form. Then the *be* affects the form of the next verb, the main verb *observe*, which appears in its present participle form, *observing*.

What happens if a sentence has all three kinds of helping verbs? The pattern still remains the same, as you can see in the next set of examples:
20. They **should** have been seeing the doctor regularly.
21. You **might** have been observing the situation more closely.

The modal, which is the first helping verb (in bold), causes *have* to be in its base form. The *have* helping verb (underlined) causes the next verb, *be*, to appear in its past participle form, that is, with the *-en* suffix (also underlined), and *be* (with a squiggly line) causes the next verb, the main verb, to be in its present participle form, that is, ending in *-ing* (also with a squiggly line).

So the overall pattern is completely consistent, whether a sentence has one, two, or three helping verbs.

As we've seen, when progressive *be* is the helping verb, the next verb always has *-ing* added to it. But sometimes verbs ending in the *-ing* suffix have a different use, as we can see in these next sentences:
22. Skiing energizes me.
23. I love cooking.

In these sentences, the *-ing* word does not follow the helping verb *be*. Instead, the *-ing* ending changes the verb into a noun. In fact, notice that the *-ing* word can be replaced with a typical noun in these sentences, for example: *Sugar energizes me*, *I love Mary*. A noun that consists of a verb and the suffix *-ing* is called a gerund.

> **Quick tip 36.4**
>
> A noun that consists of a verb and the suffix *-ing* is called a gerund. Example: *Entertain-ing is fun*.

Here are some more examples of sentences with gerunds:
24. Reading is one of life's pleasures.
25. Thinking can be hard work!
26. The criminal admitted lying.
27. They stopped worrying about it.

## Test yourself 36.4

Decide if each underlined word ending in *-ing* in the following sentences is being used as a verb, part of the progressive *be* "package," or as a noun, that is, as a gerund. To help you decide, see whether or not the *-ing* word follows the helping verb *be*.

## Lesson 36: The suffixes of auxiliary verbs

| | Verb (progressive) | Noun (gerund) |
|---|---|---|
| Sample: She likes <u>walking</u> the dog. | | ✗ |

***Getting started*** (answers on p. 166)

1. They are <u>constructing</u> small homes in that part of town.
2. He was <u>looking</u> for Jonas.
3. The candidate thought about <u>refusing</u>.
4. <u>Giving</u> to charity is an old American tradition.
5. I should have thought of <u>responding</u> earlier.

***More practice*** (answers on the website)

6. Last night we were <u>having</u> lots of fun.
7. The employee was <u>being</u> honest with you.
8. She enjoys <u>listening</u> to her iPod.
9. Some doctors recommend <u>taking</u> vitamin pills.
10. I am <u>considering</u> your offer seriously.

Here is a summary of the three helping verbs we've discussed in this lesson and the form of the verb that follows each:

| Helping verb | Following verb |
|---|---|
| modal | base form |
| perfect *have* | past participle form (typically ending in *-ed* or *-en*) |
| progressive *be*: | present participle form (always ending in *-ing*) |

Two additional helping verbs will be discussed in Lessons 52 and 53.

# Lesson 37: Tense

The verb of a sentence gives information about tense. Speakers of English generally are aware that, for example, the verb *studies* is a present tense form while the verb *studied* is a past tense form.

## Test yourself 37.1

For each verb below, decide if it is in its present tense or past tense form.

|  | Present tense | Past tense |
|---|---|---|
| Sample: was |  | x |

**Getting started** (answers on p. 167)

1. sends
2. felt
3. perceived
4. am
5. has

**More practice** (answers on the website)

6. wrote
7. sat
8. walk
9. arose
10. sing

It's important to understand that grammatical tense and real world time are not necessarily the same. Take a look at the following sentences:

1. She studied yesterday.
2. She was studying yesterday.

In sentences 1 and 2, the tense of the underlined verbs, as seen in their forms, is past; the time that is being talked about is also past. So in these cases tense and time are the same.

Now consider the following sentences:

3. I am going to France next summer.
4. She has bought the books for the course.

In sentences 3 and 4, the grammatical tense of the underlined verbs is present. (If these verbs were past tense forms, they would be *was* and *had*, respectively). However, the real-life or actual time that sentence 3 is talking about is in the future; the actual time that sentence 4 is talking about is in the past. So in sentences 3 and 4 we can see that grammatical tense and real-life time are not always the same.

For the rest of this lesson, we'll be focusing on the tense (grammatical form) and not the real-life time of English verbs.

> **Quick tip 37.1**
>
> Time refers to a point in real life at which something occurs. Tense refers to the grammatical form of a verb.

## Lesson 37: Tense

In a simple sentence, tense information is carried by only one verb. If a sentence has helping verbs as well as a main verb, which verb shows tense? In each of the sentences below, the verb that carries the tense information is underlined.

5. John <u>studies</u>.
6. John <u>studied</u>.
7. John <u>has</u> studied.
8. John <u>had</u> studied.
9. John <u>is</u> studying.
10. John <u>was</u> studying.
11. John <u>has</u> been studying.
12. John <u>had</u> been studying.

You can see that in each sentence it is the very first verb that carries the tense information, regardless of whether it's a helping verb or the main verb.

You will notice that we have not included in our list of sentences in 5 through 12 examples of sentences whose first verb is a modal. (Recall from Lesson 34 that modals always come first in sentences with more than one verb.) That is because in general, modals do not carry clear tense information. Look at the following examples:

13. I <u>might</u> do it right now / today.
14. I <u>might</u> do it tomorrow.
15. I <u>might</u> have done it yesterday.

As you can see, the form of the modal is the same (*might*), regardless of whether it refers to time in the present (sentence 13), time in the future (sentence 14), or time in the past (sentence 15). We will consider modals to be tenseless.

> **Quick tip 37.2**
>
> Tense information is always indicated by the first verb in the sentence, excluding modals.

Traditionally, sentences have been grouped into different types, according to the tense of the verb. Let's compare the following two sentences:

16. John studies every day.
17. John studied every day.

You can see that the only difference between sentence 16 and sentence 17 is that in 16, *study* is in its present tense form and in 17 *study* is in its past tense form. On this basis, sentence 16 has present tense (or simple present tense), while sentence 17 has past tense (or simple past tense).

Here are some more examples, with the verbs underlined:

18. Ira <u>sighed</u> in relief.    (past)
19. Alice <u>sees</u> her often.    (present)
20. He <u>laughed</u> hysterically.    (past)
21. I often <u>forget</u> the answer.    (present)

> **Quick tip 37.3**
>
> Sentences with no helping verb are in either the present or past tense, depending on the form of the verb.

Almost all verbs, like the verbs in sentences 18 and 20, form their past tense by adding the suffix *-ed*. These verbs are called regular verbs. Some verbs, however, do not follow this

# UNIT 12: AUXILIARY PHRASES

pattern. These verbs are called **irregular verbs**. Some examples of irregular verbs are: *see* (past tense *saw*), *write* (past tense *wrote*), and *hit* (past tense *hit*).

## Test yourself 37.2

Decide if each sentence is in the present or past tense. You'll need to find the verb to make this decision.
Sample: Her daughter giggled happily.           past

***Getting started*** (answers on p. 167)

1. They deliver furniture on Tuesdays.
2. The senator supports that bill.
3. I voted for him.
4. I ate a sandwich for lunch.
5. The shortstop hit a home run.

***More practice*** (answers on the website)

6. Michigan State beat Ohio State.
7. Our niece studies anthropology.
8. The weather is humid today.
9. The repairman arrived at noon.
10. My daughter came for a visit.

The next two sentences have **future tense** (or **simple future tense**): they have the modal helping verb *will*, followed by the base of the main verb.
   22. John <u>will</u> study tomorrow.
   23. Jessica <u>will</u> visit her soon.

> **Quick tip 37.4**
>
> Sentences with *will* followed by the main verb are in the future tense.

The future tense can also be expressed with the modal helping verb *shall*: e.g. *John shall study tomorrow*. *Shall* has restricted usage in American English: generally, it's used only in formal speech styles. Consequently, we'll ignore *shall* in our discussion here.

## Test yourself 37.3

Decide if each sentence below is in the present, past, or future tense.
Sample: Those Halloween decorations will look scary.           future

***Getting started*** (answers on p. 167)

1. He sleeps late on weekends.
2. Zach was proud of his son.
3. Bethany will get married soon.

## Lesson 37: Tense

4. The show began promptly at 8 P.M.

5. My sister will run in the New York City marathon.

***More practice*** (answers on the website)

6. The coffee tasted bitter.
7. I study in England every summer.
8. My younger brother beat me at chess.
9. Stu gets up at 7 A.M. every morning.
10. We will hold a family reunion in July.

As we saw above (in sentences 4, 11, and 12), sentences with the *have* helping verb also change in form to indicate tense:

24. I have bought the books.
25. I had bought the books.

The difference between the two sentences is that sentence 24 is in the present tense, while sentence 25 is in the past tense. Notice that it is only the form of *have* that changes to indicate the tense information. The verb after *have* is always in its past participle form, which does not change to indicate tense. Although sentences with the *have* helping verb are in the perfect aspect, when we talk about a sentence with both tense and aspect, we just use the term "tense." So therefore sentence 24 is in the present perfect tense while sentence 25 is in the past perfect tense.

> **Quick tip 37.5**
>
> If a sentence has a form of *have* as a helping verb, it will have the word *perfect* as part of the name of its tense.

> **Quick tip 37.6**
>
> The present tense forms of *have* are *have* and *has*. The past tense form of *have* is *had*.

## Test yourself 37.4

Decide if each sentence is in the present perfect or past perfect tense. Use the form of *have* to help you make your decision.

Sample: I had believed every word of that broadcast.  past perfect

***Getting started*** (answers on p. 167)

1. She had wanted to do everything her way.
2. Martha has known about the surprise.
3. Samantha had decided to do that.
4. I have written to him about that issue.
5. You have been a good friend.

UNIT 12: AUXILIARY PHRASES

*More practice* (answers on the website)

6. They have purchased a new home.
7. On our trip, we had converted $200 to euros.
8. Andy has promised to tell the truth.
9. The detective had found an important witness.
10. The Democrats have won the presidency.

What do you think is the tense of the following sentences?
26. John <u>will</u> <u>have</u> studied by then.
27. It <u>will</u> <u>have</u> been an easy test.

Since these sentences have both *will* and a form of *have* as helping verbs, they are in the future perfect tense.

> **Quick tip 37.7**
>
> If a sentence has *will* as a helping verb, it will have the word *future* as part of the name of its tense.

## Test yourself 37.5

Decide if each sentence below is in the present perfect, past perfect, or future perfect tense. Look at the form of *have* and for the presence or absence of *will* to help you.

Sample: Our friends have dropped by.                    present perfect

*Getting started* (answers on p. 167)

1. They have finished the assignment.
2. The alarm clock will have gone off by then.
3. Linda had locked the door.
4. My friend John has been a great help to me.
5. By then, I will have finished studying.

*More practice* (answers on the website)

6. Frank had appeared in a movie once.
7. You have encouraged me many times.
8. She has written a letter to her sister.
9. There had been a flood of inquiries.
10. You will have left a great legacy to your children.

## Lesson 37: Tense

Last, we come to sentences with a form of *be* as a helping verb. These also change in form to indicate tense:

28. I am buying the book.
29. I was buying the book.

The difference between the two sentences is that sentence 28 is in the present tense, while sentence 29 is in the past tense. Notice that the verb after *be* is in its present participle form (that is, its *-ing* form), which does not change to indicate tense. Remember that although sentences with the *be* helping verb are in the progressive aspect, when we talk about a sentence with both tense and aspect, we just use the term "tense." So therefore sentence 28 is in the present progressive tense while sentence 29 is in the past progressive tense.

As you might expect, the following sentences are in the future progressive tense:

30. I will be leaving at three o'clock.
31. Harry will be running the marathon.

You can see that they have both *will* and *be* as helping verbs.

> **Quick tip 37.8**
>
> If a sentence has a form of *be* as a helping verb, it will have the word *progressive* as part of the name of its tense.

> **Quick tip 37.9**
>
> The present tense forms of *be* are *am, is,* and *are*. The past tense forms of *be* are *was* and *were*.

## Test yourself 37.6

Decide if each sentence below is in the present progressive, past progressive, or future progressive tense. Look at the form of *be* and for the presence or absence of *will* to help you.
Sample: He was racing down the steps of the library.                    past progressive

***Getting started*** (answers on p. 167)

1. She is packing her bags.
2. Tom will be thinking about it all day.
3. The computer was working on it.
4. It will be snowing tomorrow.
5. I am getting tired.

***More practice*** (answers on the website)

6. They were buying stamps at the post office.
7. Jackie will be starting a new business.
8. You surely are kidding.
9. The mechanic was washing his car.
10. We will be celebrating for hours.

# UNIT 12: AUXILIARY PHRASES

Since sentences can have more than one helping verb (see Lesson 35), their tenses can have combinations of the words *present*, *past*, *future*, *perfect*, and *progressive* in their names. Here are examples of each of the possible tenses:
- 32. Mary speaks to everyone. (present)
- 33. Mary spoke to everyone. (past)
- 34. Mary will speak to everyone. (future)
- 35. Mary has spoken to everyone. (present perfect)
- 36. Mary had spoken to everyone. (past perfect)
- 37. Mary will have spoken to everyone. (future perfect)
- 38. Mary is speaking to everyone. (present progressive)
- 39. Mary was speaking to everyone. (past progressive)
- 40. Mary will be speaking to everyone. (future progressive)
- 41. Mary has been speaking to everyone. (present perfect progressive)
- 42. Mary had been speaking to everyone. (past perfect progressive)
- 43. Mary will have been speaking to everyone. (future perfect progressive)

To sum up:
(a) A sentence with *will* always has the word *future* in its tense name.
(b) A sentence with a *have* helping verb always has the word *perfect* in its tense name.
(c) A sentence with a *be* helping verb followed by a verb in its *-ing* form always has the word *progressive* in its tense name.
(d) For sentences without *will*, look at the form of the first helping verb, if there is one, or of the main verb, if there's no helping verb, to decide if the tense is present or past.

## Test yourself 37.7

Identify the tense name of each of the verb combinations below.
Sample: had thought    past perfect

***Getting started*** (answers on p. 168)

1. will consider
2. experienced
3. will have wanted
4. had been watching
5. will be reading

***More practice*** (answers on the website)

6. were acting
7. will have been studying
8. has had
9. have been sleeping
10. mention

## Test yourself 37.8

Identify the tense name of each of the sentences below.
Sample: He will be expecting great things of her.          future progressive

***Getting started*** (answers on p. 168)

1. She was making some progress.
2. Marie shrugged her shoulders.
3. She will be taking a long walk.
4. He has had two serious operations.
5. They had been getting numerous phone calls.

*Lesson 37: Tense*

***More practice*** (answers on the website)

6. Neil is going to Washington tomorrow.
7. Clare has been watching ESPN for years.
8. You will be a champion one day.
9. Luis will have worked for IBM for 40 years.
10. I will have been sleeping for nine hours.

# Answer keys: *Test yourself, Getting started* questions – Unit 12

## Test yourself 31.1

|   | Helping verb: NO | Helping verb: YES |
|---|---|---|
| 1. They were arguing loudly. |  | ✗ |
| 2. The frog had jumped five feet. |  | ✗ |
| 3. You invited everyone. | ✗ |  |
| 4. I must buy some milk. |  | ✗ |
| 5. Harry lives in Europe. | ✗ |  |

## Test yourself 31.2

|   | Helping verb: NO | Helping verb: YES |
|---|---|---|
| 1. You might write her a letter. |  | ✗ |
| 2. Congress voted on the bill. | ✗ |  |
| 3. Beth has survived that ordeal. |  | ✗ |
| 4. I could be an actor. |  | ✗ |
| 5. The Giants won the Super Bowl. | ✗ |  |

## Test yourself 32.1

1. They must delay the invasion.
2. You will find courage in your heart.
3. Mr. Knight might go with you.
4. You should be proud of yourself.
5. Tomorrow we may go to the movies.

## Test yourself 32.2

1. The curtains might hide the view.
2. Paul could work on the problem.
3. She can leave this afternoon.
4. You must go to the emergency room immediately.
5. The children will enjoy these gifts.

## Test yourself 33.1

1. The bridge had collapsed.
2. That cheerful woman has saved the day.
3. My uncles have visited us every summer.
4. Her neighbor has been an attorney for twenty years.
5. Suzie had traveled to Belgium twice before.

## Test yourself 33.2

1. Joan and Sam have worked for hours.
2. Their mother has spoken of you often.
3. The prime minister had written to him.
4. Your daughter has grown a lot taller.
5. She has seen her friends twice since last Sunday.

## Test yourself 33.3

|  | Helping verb | Main verb |
|---|---|---|
| 1. Jack has experienced a good time. | ✗ |  |
| 2. He has seen her often. | ✗ |  |
| 3. You have a lot of DVDs. |  | ✗ |
| 4. She had tacos for dinner. |  | ✗ |
| 5. Your professor has the answer to your question. |  | ✗ |

## Test yourself 34.1

1. The reporter was writing her story.
2. He is controlling his temper.
3. You are learning about syntax.
4. They were watching a movie last Sunday.
5. I am doing a lot of things right now.

## Test yourself 34.2

1. I was talking to Harry.
2. Irving and Annie are studying Latin.
3. He is testing her loyalty.
4. I am taking a walk.
5. You were reading for hours.

## Test yourself 34.3

|  | Helping verb | Main verb |
|---|---|---|
| 1. Sam is looking at the mail. | ✗ |  |
| 2. That concept was difficult. |  | ✗ |
| 3. You are helping her a lot. | ✗ |  |
| 4. I am a doctor. |  | ✗ |
| 5. They were watching TV. | ✗ |  |

## Test yourself 35.1

1. She was focusing on the mirror. ....1....
2. Andy should have been enjoying his new career. ....3....
3. Mrs. Packard's life changed at that point. ....0....
4. You can have two scoops of ice cream. ....1....
5. I might have committed a serious error. ....2....

## Test yourself 35.2

1. You should read this book.
2. She had been greeting me happily.

## UNIT 12: AUXILIARY PHRASES

3. Janice might have gotten the flu.
4. My question was bothering him.
5. The prime suspect might have been telling the truth.

### Test yourself 35.3

1. I had been writing to him often.
2. Their mother has spoken of you a lot.
3. Sam will recognize it immediately.
4. We were good friends. (No helping verb.)
5. You should be studying right now.

### Test yourself 35.4

1. They can do the research.
2. Suzanne might be leaving sooner.
3. Papa has been teasing him.
4. I might have been being too cautious.
5. The plane was late.

### Test yourself 36.1

1. She is leaving on the ten o'clock train.
2. The curtains were masking the view.
3. I was wondering about his behavior.
4. Paul is leaning on his wife's chair.
5. They are sounding rather defensive.

### Test yourself 36.2

1. The women had spoken to each other recently.
2. Unfortunately, the heroine had married the villain.
3. Andy and George have enjoyed themselves enormously.
4. My student has written an interesting essay on technology.
5. The hockey game has ended in a tie.

### Test yourself 36.3

1. Richard will believe the truth.
2. The waiter might bring it.
3. They may be home late.
4. We shall overcome this obstacle.
5. I would do it in an instant.

### Test yourself 36.4

| | Verb (progressive) | Noun (gerund) |
|---|---|---|
| 1. They are constructing small homes in that part of town. | ✗ | |
| 2. He was looking for Jonas. | ✗ | |
| 3. The candidate thought about refusing. | | ✗ |
| 4. Giving to charity is an old American tradition. | | ✗ |
| 5. I should have thought of responding earlier. | | ✗ |

Answer keys: Unit 12

## Test yourself 37.1

|   | Present tense | Past tense |
|---|---|---|
| 1. sends | x | |
| 2. felt | | x |
| 3. perceived | | x |
| 4. am | x | |
| 5. has | x | |

## Test yourself 37.2

1. They deliver furniture on Tuesdays.   present
2. The senator supports that bill.   present
3. I voted for him.   past
4. I ate a sandwich for lunch.   past
5. The shortstop hit a home run.   past

## Test yourself 37.3

1. He sleeps late on weekends.   present
2. Zach was proud of his son.   past
3. Bethany will get married soon.   future
4. The show began promptly at 8 P.M.   past
5. My sister will run in the New York City marathon.   future

## Test yourself 37.4

1. She had wanted to do everything her way.   past perfect
2. Martha has known about the surprise.   present perfect
3. Samantha had decided to do that.   past perfect
4. I have written to him about that issue.   present perfect
5. You have been a good friend.   present perfect

## Test yourself 37.5

1. They have finished the assignment.   present perfect
2. The alarm clock will have gone off by then.   future perfect
3. Linda had locked the door.   past perfect
4. My friend John has been a great help to me.   present perfect
5. By then, I will have finished studying.   future perfect

## Test yourself 37.6

1. She is packing her bags.   present progressive
2. Tom will be thinking about it all day.   future progressive
3. The computer was working on it.   past progressive
4. It will be snowing tomorrow.   future progressive
5. I am getting tired.   present progressive

# UNIT 12: AUXILIARY PHRASES

## Test yourself 37.7

1. will consider — future
2. experienced — past
3. will have wanted — future perfect
4. had been watching — past perfect progressive
5. will be reading — future progressive

## Test yourself 37.8

1. She was making some progress. — past progressive
2. Marie shrugged her shoulders. — past
3. She will be taking a long walk. — future progressive
4. He has had two serious operations. — present perfect
5. They had been getting numerous phone calls. — past perfect progressive

☞ **FOR A REVIEW EXERCISE OF THIS UNIT, SEE THE WEBSITE.**

# UNIT 13: SUBJECTS AND OBJECTS

Sentences may contain several noun phrases. These noun phrases can have different jobs, or functions, within the sentence. Take a look at the following sentence:

On Valentine's Day, <u>my brother</u> bought <u>a bouquet of flowers</u> for <u>his wife</u>.

The underlined noun phrases are doing different things: *my brother* is doing the action, *a bouquet of flowers* is receiving the action, and *his wife* is receiving the flowers. In the lessons of this unit, we discuss in detail these grammatical functions (or grammatical relations).

# Lesson 38: Subjects

We can identify the subject of a sentence with an action verb (see Lesson 9) by answering the question: "Who is doing the action?" For example, in the sentence *Confucius spoke many words of wisdom*, the action is *speaking*. Who is, or was, doing the speaking? *Confucius*. *Confucius* is therefore the subject of the sentence. The subjects are underlined in the following examples:
 1. <u>John</u> baked a cake.
 2. <u>You</u> are going to grin and bear it.
 3. Just then, <u>the children</u> walked in.
 4. <u>He</u> delivered a small package.
 5. <u>Mr. Bucknose</u>, the carpenter, sleeps in the spare room.
 6. Wearily, <u>the group</u> trudged onward.
 7. <u>I</u> usually take a nap in the afternoon.

Generally, the subject is at or near the beginning of the sentence. More specifically, the subject is the first noun phrase (see Lesson 28) in the sentence.

> **Quick tip 38.1**
>
> If the main verb of the sentence is an action verb, the subject of the sentence is the doer of the action and generally comes before the verb. It can be found by answering the question: "Who or what is doing the action?"

## Test yourself 38.1

Underline the subject in each of the sentences below. In these sentences, it will always be the doer of the action and will be the first noun phrase in the sentence.
Sample: <u>Jeanette</u> demanded an answer to her question.

*Getting started* (answers on p. 189)

1. The servant accompanied His Lordship.
2. Jean participated in the Tour de France.
3. Such families have often preferred to travel in style.
4. They could do nothing except run.
5. Mr. Tower quietly explained all this to his son.

*More practice* (answers on the website)

6. The diners are arguing loudly.
7. Your uncle invited me to accompany him on his business trip.
8. The Yankees won the World Series many times.
9. Macy's is holding a huge sale next Sunday.
10. The TV repairman has just arrived.

---

The subject is underlined in the following sentences:
 8. <u>John</u> is tall.
 9. <u>That church</u> is impressive.

*Lesson 38: Subjects*

    10. Both brothers became architects.
    11. Earlier, she had felt dizzy.

In these sentences, the subject is not performing an action – the verb is not an action verb. Rather, the verb is a linking verb (see Lesson 9). When the verb in the sentence is a linking verb, the subject can be found by asking the question: "Who or what is this sentence about?" In these cases, the subject is found at or near the beginning of the sentence, before the verb.

> **Quick tip 38.2**
>
> If the main verb of the sentence is a linking verb, the subject is who or what the sentence is about; the subject is found before the verb.

## Test yourself 38.2

Underline the subject in each of the sentences below. In these sentences, it will always be who or what the sentence is about and will be the first noun phrase in the sentence.
Sample: The professor was imprisoned for his beliefs.

***Getting started*** (answers on p. 189)

1. The Hotel Regina is an attractive place.
2. It became the best-known symbol of Paris.
3. The local merchants were on his side.
4. Charles looked thoughtful.
5. Christine seemed insecure.

***More practice*** (answers on the website)

6. She was determined to meet Dr. Richards again.
7. His older sister resembled her father, unfortunately.
8. Her folks are good people.
9. My son is destined for success as an attorney.
10. Their apology seems genuine.

## Test yourself 38.3

Underline the subject in each of the sentences below. In these sentences, it will either be the doer of the action or who or what the sentence is about. The subject will be the first noun phrase in the sentence.
Sample: These proportions are inaccurate.

***Getting started*** (answers on p. 189)

1. The editor looked for new ideas for the magazine.
2. You can rely on the experts at that company.
3. Maggie usually goes berry picking in the summer.
4. Roger is happy with his new computer.
5. The workers went on strike for a couple of weeks.

***More practice*** (answers on the website)

6. Alana's hair smells fresh.
7. I got there on time.
8. They postponed the ball game on account of bad weather.
9. Bowling is a favorite pastime of mine.
10. Some students missed the final exam.

The subject is not always right at the beginning of the sentence:
    12. In the afternoon, I usually take a nap.
    13. In truth, Don Diego had never really had a career.

# UNIT 13: SUBJECTS AND OBJECTS

14. That day, <u>his timing</u> was perfect.
15. When in the country, <u>Jack</u> was up before dawn.

In each of these sentences, the subject is preceded by an adverb (see Lesson 27) or adverbial clause, a group of words typically giving information about time, place, or manner.

## Test yourself 38.4

Underline the subject in each of the sentences below. The subject will not necessarily be the first noun phrase in the sentence.

Sample: By late afternoon, <u>he</u> is usually exhausted.

***Getting started*** (answers on p. 189)

1. After that, their neighbor came more often to help them.
2. Fortunately, that university program is accredited.
3. In the morning, I'm planting those flowers.
4. Eventually, Mr. Mulligan broke the silence.
5. While running for office, the candidate campaigned vigorously.

***More practice*** (answers on the website)

6. Generally speaking, they don't know many foreign languages.
7. Dr. Wright's chauffeur drove him to the clinic.
8. For many reasons, Michael prefers to live in the suburbs.
9. This movie lasted a long time.
10. Exciting times are much more memorable than boring ones.

# Lesson 39: Direct objects

As we saw in Lesson 38, a noun phrase can function as the subject of a sentence. A noun phrase can also have other functions. For example, a noun phrase may be acted upon by the subject and follow the verb. These noun phrases are called direct objects. The direct objects in the sentences below are underlined:
1. John baked a cake.
2. Leah had visualized a simple room.
3. She is buying a small studio apartment.
4. My niece rented a movie last night.

How can you tell which noun phrase in a sentence functions as the direct object? In general, the direct object is the answer to the questions: "Who or what is being acted upon? Who or what is receiving the action?" Thus, for example, in the sentence *My niece rented a movie last night*, the direct object is *a movie*, since *a movie* is what is being acted upon (being rented). Typically, direct objects occur immediately after the verb. (We discuss a different pattern in Lesson 40.)

> **Quick tip 39.1**
>
> The direct object of a sentence is receiving the action. It can usually be found by answering the question: "Who or what is being acted upon or receiving the action?" The direct object typically occurs immediately after the verb.

## Test yourself 39.1

Underline the direct object in each of the sentences below. Be sure to ask yourself who or what is being acted upon or receiving the action.
Sample: I saw a statue in the museum.

***Getting started*** (answers on p. 189)

1. You must include all relevant facts.
2. Bridget is asking numerous questions.
3. The Spanish ships needed fresh supplies.
4. She will watch the baby.
5. The townspeople have wanted tax relief for years.

***More practice*** (answers on the website)

6. Most people greeted us warmly at the reception.
7. I bought two bottles of Pepsi.
8. Actors must memorize their lines.
9. Last week, Jack renewed his passport.
10. Where did you get that sweater?

Not all sentences have direct objects. Here are examples of sentences with action verbs that do not have direct objects.

# UNIT 13: SUBJECTS AND OBJECTS

     5. My friend laughed loudly.
     6. Mr. Thomas slept well.
     7. You're always worrying.

You may remember, from Lesson 10, that there are transitive and intransitive verbs. Transitive verbs, like *bake* or *rent*, act on something or someone and so they have direct objects. Intransitive verbs, like *laugh*, *sleep*, and *worry*, aren't acting upon something or someone and so don't have direct objects.

    What about these next sentences?

       8. My friend stopped <u>at the grocery store</u>.
       9. Mr. Thomas slept well <u>during the night</u>.
     10. You're always worrying <u>about something</u>.

As you can see, these sentences have prepositional phrases, which are underlined (Lesson 29). A prepositional phrase is <u>not</u> a direct object. For example, *at the grocery store* in sentence 8 and *during the night* in sentence 9 are not being acted upon.

    To sum up, only transitive action verbs have direct objects, and prepositional phrases are not direct objects.

## Test yourself 39.2

Decide whether or not each sentence below has a direct object.

|  | Direct object? Yes | No |
|---|---|---|
| Sample: Her best friend entered the room first. | **x** | |

***Getting started*** (answers on p. 190)

| | | |
|---|---|---|
| 1. We'll discuss each argument. | | |
| 2. Carter worked for a lumber company. | | |
| 3. Those gamblers are losing their money. | | |
| 4. At 7 P.M. we left for the theater. | | |
| 5. The children are enjoying Disneyland. | | |

***More practice*** (answers on the website)

| | | |
|---|---|---|
| 6. I slept well last night. | | |
| 7. They watch football on Sunday nights. | | |
| 8. Jill and Sam have left with a friend. | | |
| 9. Can you pass the butter, please? | | |
| 10. She wants a big scoop of chocolate ice cream. | | |

    What about this next sentence?

       11. She *is* a doctor.

Is *a doctor* receiving the action of *is*? Kind of a strange question, isn't it? That's because *is* is not an action verb; it's a linking verb (see Lesson 9). Sentences with linking verbs don't have direct objects, since there is no action happening in the sentence. In each sentence below, the linking verb is italicized. The underlined portion of each sentence is not a direct object, since it's not being acted upon. Instead, it's called the **verb complement**.

## Lesson 39: Direct objects

12. My teacher *resembles* Tom Cruise.
13. That dinner *was* delicious.
14. Her husband *became* a lawyer.

## Test yourself 39.3

Decide if the underlined phrase in each sentence below is a direct object or a verb complement. To make this decision, you can: (1) ask yourself if something or someone is being acted upon, and/or (2) decide if the verb is an action or linking verb.

Sample: Bill became a member of the President's cabinet.     verb complement

***Getting started*** (answers on p. 190)

1. Gerald has taken that course.
2. Rob used this technique in his restaurant.
3. Adam might withdraw his resignation.
4. The mayor is sounding confident.
5. We quickly got ready.

***More practice*** (answers on the website)

6. He was getting a pastrami sandwich in the deli.
7. She loves her new car
8. We were best friends in high school.
9. I'll take you to the movies.
10. He feels foolish.

## Test yourself 39.4

Underline the direct objects in the sentences below. Not all sentences will have a direct object.
Sample: I put the letter in his mailbox.

***Getting started*** (answers on p. 190)

1. Our discussion was highly entertaining.
2. He had a growing family.
3. She quickly got indignant.
4. You must be the new baby sitter.
5. The sheriff arrested a suspect in the fraud investigation.

***More practice*** (answers on the website)

6. The coach of the University of Texas football team is replacing his quarterback.
7. They walked in the woods till sunset.
8. I proposed some tentative solutions.
9. He confessed on the second day of the trial.
10. Our plane had left on time.

## Test yourself 39.5

Underline the subjects and put a squiggly line under the direct objects in the sentences below.
Sample: His company was losing millions.

## UNIT 13: SUBJECTS AND OBJECTS

***Getting started*** (answers on p. 190)

1. The soldiers fired their weapons.
2. A talented designer made that hat.
3. She had married her next-door neighbor.
4. Maria was watching her favorite soap opera.
5. These people really irritate me.

***More practice*** (answers on the website)

6. Sonya has found the directions to the party.
7. He added salt to his soup.
8. The contestant had to make a difficult decision.
9. Rhonda is expecting her third child.
10. Last week, Martin's friends bought a present for his birthday.

# Lesson 40: Indirect objects

Sometimes a noun phrase is the answer to the question: "Who or what is receiving the direct object?" This noun phrase is called the indirect object. The indirect objects are underlined in the sentences below.
1. Mary gave the information to Robert.
2. She told the truth to her granddaughter.
3. They bought a car for their teenage daughter.
4. The accountant is giving a present to her husband.

So in sentence 4, for instance, the noun phrase *a present* is the direct object and the noun phrase *her husband* is the indirect object, since *her husband* is receiving *the present*, the direct object.

> **Quick tip 40.1**
>
> The indirect object of a sentence can be found by answering the question: "Who or what is receiving the direct object?"

You can see that sentences that have indirect objects must also have direct objects, since indirect objects receive direct objects. The opposite is not true: sentences with direct objects don't necessarily have indirect objects.

A direct object and an indirect object each follows the verb and is referred to by the term **object**. The term object can also refer to objects of a preposition, that is, noun phrases that follow prepositions. (See Lesson 29.)

## Test yourself 40.1

Underline the indirect object in each of the sentences below.
Sample: Jane baked the cake for Grant.

***Getting started*** (answers on p. 190)

1. Holly left the plate for Luke.
2. She taught the principles to the class.
3. Big Bird is telling the story to all the children.
4. His father had bought the boat for Jonathan.
5. You will show the money to me.

***More practice*** (answers on the website)

6. Jamie's friend sent a text message to her.
7. They bid farewell to their house guests.
8. The teenage idol is throwing a party for his fans.
9. I want to wish good luck to you.
10. My dad baked a pie for us.

Indirect objects are introduced by the preposition *to* or *for*. Some verbs, such as *tell* and *show*, use *to* to introduce an indirect object, while some verbs, such as *buy* and *leave*, use *for*.

# UNIT 13: SUBJECTS AND OBJECTS

*To* and *for* do not function only to introduce indirect objects; often, *to* and *for* have other functions. Take a look at these next sentences and notice the differences between them:

5. Mary gave the baby to Robert.
6. Mary carried the baby to the corner.

In both sentences, *Mary* is the subject, the doer of the action, and *the baby* is the direct object, the receiver of the action. In sentence 5, *Robert* is receiving *the baby*, the direct object, so *Robert* is the indirect object. However, in sentence 6 *the corner* is not receiving *the baby* and so it's not the indirect object. (It's the object of the preposition *to*; see Lesson 29.)

Here's a similar pair of sentences:

7. He got a gift for his wife.
8. He got a gift for his birthday.

In both sentences, *He* is the subject, the doer of the action, and *a gift* is the direct object, the receiver of the action. In sentence 7, *his wife* is receiving *a gift*, the direct object, so *his wife* is the indirect object. However, in sentence 8 *his birthday* is not receiving *a gift*, so it's not the indirect object. (It's the object of the preposition *for*.)

## Test yourself 40.2

For each of the sentences below, indicate whether or not *to* and *for* are being used to introduce an indirect object. Ask yourself if the noun phrase following *to* or *for* is receiving the direct object.

|  | Introducing an indirect object? | |
|---|---|---|
|  | Yes | No |
| Sample: I inspected the car for dents. |  | ✗ |

*Getting started* (answers on p. 190)

1. John worked that job for fifty years.
2. The professor is showing the problem to the student.
3. His wife and child brought fruit to him at the hospital.
4. Tom has left the company for another job.
5. The visiting king thanked the president for his hospitality.

*More practice* (answers on the website)

6. She sent the e-mail to her sister.
7. We will remember this general for his heroism.
8. I have forwarded your message to your mother.
9. He took his friend to the theater.
10. The Black family took a ride to the countryside.

Here are sentences 1–4 again, but this time with a "partner" sentence:

9a. Mary gave the information to Robert.
9b. Mary gave Robert the information.

*Lesson 40: Indirect objects*

10a. She told the truth to her granddaughter.
10b. She told her granddaughter the truth.
11a. They bought a car for their teenage daughter.
11b. They bought their teenage daughter a car.
12a. The accountant is giving a present to him.
12b. The accountant is giving him a present.

You can see that in the second sentence of each pair, the indirect object has moved so that it comes before the direct object, rather than after it. English gives us two choices for the position of indirect objects: (a) the indirect object can occur after the direct object (which follows the verb), with *to* or *for* introducing it, or (b) the indirect object can occur before the direct object (and after the verb), without *to* or *for*.

> **Quick tip 40.2**
>
> An indirect object can occur: (a) after the direct object (which follows the verb), with *to* or *for* introducing it, or (b) before the direct object (and after the verb), without *to* or *for*. For example: *Joan gave a present to Bill* or *Joan gave Bill a present*. (*Bill* is the indirect object in both sentences.)

> **Quick tip 40.3**
>
> To help you decide if a sentence has an indirect object, see if the sentence can be changed from a pattern like *The boys left a note for their teacher* to a sentence with a pattern like *The boys left their teacher a note*, or vice versa.

Note that when the direct object is a pronoun, the two patterns are not both possible, as you can see in these next sentence pairs:

13a. Her best friend bought it for her family.
13b. *Her best friend bought her family it.
14a. Lucy sold them to her neighbor.
14b. *Lucy sold her neighbor them.

That is, when the direct object is a pronoun, it must come before the indirect object.

> **Quick tip 40.4**
>
> If the direct object is a pronoun, it must come before the indirect object. Example: *My sister sent it to her friend*, *\*My sister sent her friend it.*

## Test yourself 40.3

Each sentence below contains an indirect object, which is underlined. Change each sentence to the other pattern, by moving the indirect object and either deleting or adding *to* or *for*.

Sample: Sally made us breakfast.   Sally made breakfast for us.

# UNIT 13: SUBJECTS AND OBJECTS

*Getting started* (answers on p. 191)

1. The principal might show the film to <u>her students</u>.

2. Mrs. Hausen sent <u>the company</u> her check.

3. We bought the house for <u>our parents</u>.

4. The referee threw <u>me</u> the ball.

5. The artist is drawing a sketch for <u>her patron</u>.

*More practice* (answers on the website)

6. I am saving this seat for <u>my father</u>.

7. My colleague did <u>me</u> a favor.

8. Albert passed <u>his friend</u> a note.

9. She will read <u>her children</u> a poem.

10. The boss wished much success to <u>his new employee</u>.

## Test yourself 40.4

Each sentence below contains an indirect object (not underlined). Change each sentence to the other pattern, by moving the indirect object and either deleting or adding *to* or *for*.
Sample: Steve gave Mary a package.    Steve gave a package to Mary.

*Getting started* (answers on p. 191)

1. He will send the poem to his fiancée.

Lesson 40: Indirect objects

2. The professor is e-mailing the students his comments.

3. That company built a ship for the navy.

4. She drew a picture for her son.

5. Amanda's friend was throwing a party for her.

*More practice* (answers on the website)

6. I sang a lullaby to you.

7. The company's president had shipped the order to them.

8. The librarian found George a good book.

9. The arresting officer must read his rights to him.

10. My aunt baked me my favorite dessert.

## Test yourself 40.5

Underline the indirect object in each sentence below. It can occur either before or after the direct object.
Sample: Jerry made me that bench.

*Getting started* (answers on p. 191)

1. We found a dress for her.
2. Mr. Duquesne has brought him the plans.
3. The old hunter told us the story.
4. The instructor is ordering this book for the students in his class.
5. I never promised you a rose garden.

*More practice* (answers on the website)

6. The contractor will build a brand new deck for me.
7. Can't she give him a straight answer?
8. The realtor showed them a lovely house.
9. The economist had painted a rosy picture for his audience.
10. I got you a small present.

## UNIT 13: SUBJECTS AND OBJECTS

### Test yourself 40.6

For each sentence below, underline the direct object and put a squiggly line under the indirect object, if there is one. Remember, the indirect object can occur either before or after the direct object.

Sample: That man got <u>~his friend~</u> <u>a computer</u>.

***Getting started*** (answers on p. 191)

1. The children gave the teacher an apple.
2. I brought this for you.
3. The two men clasped hands.
4. This treaty will benefit all mankind.
5. She is telling the reporter the truth.

***More practice*** (answers on the website)

6. Don't give me that!
7. We have to return this to the store.
8. At the meeting, he showed us his true colors.
9. People have been telling this story for ages.
10. I bid all of you good night.

# Lesson 41: The functions of pronouns

Now that we've talked about subjects and objects in some detail, it's a good idea for us to reexamine subject and object pronouns, which we first discussed in Lesson 21.

Take a look at the noun phrase *the teacher* in each of the sentences below.

1. The teacher went home early today.
   (*The teacher* is the subject.)
2. The students liked the teacher very much.
   (*The teacher* is the direct object.)
3. The parents gave the questionnaire to the teacher.
   (*The teacher* is the indirect object.)

Notice that *the teacher* has the same form whether it's functioning as the subject, the direct object, or the indirect object in a sentence. This is true for all nouns in English: they don't change form when they change function.

In contrast, there are subject pronouns and object pronouns (see Lesson 21). Subject pronouns are used when a pronoun is functioning as the subject of a sentence (see Lesson 38). The subject pronoun is underlined in the following sentences:

4. I read the newspaper every day.
5. She is happy.
6. We love potato chips.

Object pronouns are used in all other contexts. The three major uses for object pronouns are: direct object (Lesson 39), indirect object (Lesson 40), and object of a preposition (Lesson 29). The object pronouns are underlined in the following sentences:

7. My sister congratulated me on my birthday. (direct object)
8. The director sent her a message. (indirect object)
9. Mrs. Raffsky spoke to us on the phone. (object of a preposition)

> **Quick tip 41.1**
>
> A subject pronoun is used when it is functioning as the subject of the sentence. An object pronoun is used when it is functioning as: (a) the direct object of the sentence; (b) the indirect object of the sentence; (c) the object of a preposition.

## Test yourself 41.1

For each underlined pronoun below, indicate whether it is a subject or object pronoun. For *you* and *it*, you will need to look at how the pronoun is being used in the sentence.

|  | Subject pronoun | Object pronoun |
|---|---|---|
| Sample: I feel great. | x | |

***Getting started*** (answers on p. 191)

1. She laughed at the movie.
2. Don't bother me now.

## UNIT 13: SUBJECTS AND OBJECTS

3. I don't feel guilty.
4. He has asked her to dance.
5. Chris had been living near you.

*More practice* (answers on the website)

6. It is not a very interesting movie.
7. This does not concern us.
8. He disappointed his friends.
9. The critics were raving about it.
10. It doesn't matter to them at all.

## Test yourself 41.2

Each of the sentences below contains an object pronoun, which is underlined. Indicate whether it's being used as a direct object, an indirect object, or the object of a preposition.
Sample: Audra lives very far from him.        object of a preposition

*Getting started* (answers on p. 192)

1. My dear friend sent me a postcard from Italy.
2. A teenager sat next to me in the theater.
3. Irma has bought you the cookware.
4. The dog approached them.
5. That family is always blaming us for their problems.

*More practice* (answers on the website)

6. They gave us their promise.
7. He is renting an apartment close to me.
8. I never saw it.
9. He gave her an ultimatum.
10. Brandon will even buy it from you.

---

### To enhance your understanding

In the past, *who* and *whom* worked the same way as subject and object pronouns. In particular, *who* was used when functioning as a subject and *whom* was used when functioning as an object:

    10. Who is running away? (subject: *Who* is doing the action.)
    11. Whom does Katie like? (direct object: *Whom* is receiving the action.)

However, like all languages, English changes over time, and today, for all but the strictest traditional grammarians, *who* is used in all contexts, except when it directly follows a preposition (see below). So today a sentence like the following is perfectly grammatical:

    12. Who does Katie like? (direct object)

*Lesson 41: The functions of pronouns*

While most of us prefer to use *who* in sentence 12, it's still okay to use *whom* in these contexts. It's just not necessary to do so, and it tends to sound very formal.

Note that *whom* must be used when it follows a preposition. In the following examples, *whom* and the preposition before it are underlined.

13. With whom would you like to speak?
14. To whom may I direct your question?

# Lesson 42: Implied subjects: commands

1. Open that book right now!
2. Don't even think about crossing the street here!
3. Please be careful.

We all recognize a command when we hear one. We have seen that all sentences have a subject, but where is the subject of these commands? Speakers of English readily agree that these sentences do, in fact, have a subject. The subject, though not stated, is understood or implied to be *you*. Thus, when someone says "Wash the dishes!" you know they're talking to you. Commands are also called imperative sentences. In writing, command sentences often end with an exclamation point (!).

> **Quick tip 42.1**
>
> The subject of commands is an understood or implied *you*.

## Test yourself 42.1

Indicate the subject of each sentence below. If it's a command, specify *you* as the subject. (We won't be using exclamation points in this exercise.)

|  | *Subject* |
|---|---|
| Sample: Eat a well-balanced diet. | you |

***Getting started*** (answers on p. 192)

| | Subject |
|---|---|
| 1. These illnesses are treatable. | |
| 2. The judge had made a terrible mistake. | |
| 3. Be supportive. | |
| 4. Joan's father is an architect. | |
| 5. Stand up for your rights. | |

***More practice*** (answers on the website)

| | Subject |
|---|---|
| 6. Give me a break. | |
| 7. I can't give it to you. | |
| 8. Don't raise your voice to me. | |
| 9. Help me out with this. | |
| 10. She will be planting roses in that garden. | |

## Lesson 42: Implied subjects

### To enhance your understanding

There are a number of ways to prove what you, as a speaker of English, intuitively know: that *you* is the implicit subject of command sentences. We present one of these arguments here.

Take a look at the following sentences:
4. I held my breath.
5. You held your breath.
6. He held his breath.
7. She held her breath.

While these sentences are grammatical, the following sentences are not:
8a. *I held your breath.
8b. *I held his breath.
8c. *I held their breath.
9a. *You held my breath.
9b. *You held his breath.
9c. *You held their breath.

Can you explain why these sentences are ungrammatical? Clearly, a person cannot hold someone else's breath. Thus the two underlined pronouns must refer to the same person. If they don't, the sentence is not grammatical, as in 8 and 9 above.

Now what about commands which contain this same expression? Look at the following grammatical and ungrammatical commands:
10. Hold your breath!
11. *Hold my breath!
12. *Hold his breath!
13. *Hold their breath!

In fact, the only pronoun allowed in the command context *Hold _____ breath!* is *your*. Since we know that *your* must refer to the same person as the subject, it follows that the subject in the command must be *you*. That is, even though the *you* is not actually stated, we treat a command as though the subject were *you*.

## Test yourself 42.2

For each sentence below, indicate its subject (stated or understood), direct object, if there is one, and indirect object, if there is one.

|  | Subject | Direct Object | Indirect Object |
|---|---|---|---|
| Sample: Give the money to Harry. | you | the money | Harry |

***Getting started*** (answers on p. 192)

1. You can see marks in the dirt.
2. That film sounds interesting.
3. The congregants built the temple.
4. Give it to me!
5. We need this computer.

## UNIT 13: SUBJECTS AND OBJECTS

***More practice*** (answers on the website)

6. Don't worry about it!
7. They have been rearranging the display.
8. They sent Bill the bill.
9. Watch me!
10. Mary fell to the floor.

# Answer keys: *Test yourself, Getting started* questions – Unit 13

### Test yourself 38.1

1. The servant accompanied His Lordship.
2. Jean participated in the Tour de France.
3. Such families have often preferred to travel in style.
4. They could do nothing except run.
5. Mr. Tower quietly explained all this to his son.

### Test yourself 38.2

1. The Hotel Regina is an attractive place.
2. It became the best-known symbol of Paris.
3. The local merchants were on his side.
4. Charles looked thoughtful.
5. Christine seemed insecure.

### Test yourself 38.3

1. The editor looked for new ideas for the magazine.
2. You can rely on the experts at that company.
3. Maggie usually goes berry picking in the summer.
4. Roger is happy with his new computer.
5. The workers went on strike for a couple of weeks.

### Test yourself 38.4

1. After that, their neighbor came more often to help them.
2. Fortunately, that university program is accredited.
3. In the morning, I'm planting those flowers.
4. Eventually, Mr. Mulligan broke the silence.
5. While running for office, the candidate campaigned vigorously.

### Test yourself 39.1

1. You must include all relevant facts.
2. Bridget is asking numerous questions.
3. The Spanish ships needed fresh supplies.
4. She will watch the baby.
5. The townspeople have wanted tax relief for years.

# UNIT 13: SUBJECTS AND OBJECTS

## Test yourself 39.2

| | Direct object? Yes | No |
|---|---|---|
| 1. We'll discuss each argument. | x | |
| 2. Carter worked for a lumber company. | | x |
| 3. Those gamblers are losing their money. | x | |
| 4. At 7 P.M. we left for the theater. | | x |
| 5. The children are enjoying Disneyland. | x | |

## Test yourself 39.3

1. Gerald has taken <u>that course</u>. — direct object
2. Rob used <u>this technique</u> in his restaurant. — direct object
3. Adam might withdraw <u>his resignation</u>. — direct object
4. The mayor is sounding <u>confident</u>. — verb complement
5. We quickly got <u>ready</u>. — verb complement

## Test yourself 39.4

1. Our discussion was highly entertaining.
2. He had a growing family.
3. She quickly got indignant.
4. You must be the new baby sitter.
5. The sheriff arrested a suspect in the fraud investigation.

## Test yourself 39.5

1. The soldiers fired their weapons.
2. A talented designer made that hat.
3. She had married her next-door neighbor.
4. Maria was watching her favorite soap opera.
5. These people really irritate me.

## Test yourself 40.1

1. Holly left the plate for Luke.
2. She taught the principles to the class.
3. Big Bird is telling the story to all the children.
4. His father had bought the boat for Jonathan.
5. You will show the money to me.

## Test yourself 40.2

| | Introducing an indirect object? | |
|---|---|---|
| | Yes | No |
| 1. John worked that job for fifty years. | | x |
| 2. The professor is showing the problem to the student. | x | |
| 3. His wife and child brought fruit to him at the hospital. | x | |
| 4. Tom's has left the company for another job. | | x |
| 5. The visiting king thanked the president for his hospitality. | | x |

## Test yourself 40.3

1. The principal might show the film to <u>her students</u>.
   The principal might show her students the film.
2. Mrs. Hausen sent <u>the company</u> her check.
   Mrs. Hausen sent her check to the company.
3. We bought the house for <u>our parents</u>.
   We bought our parents the house.
4. The referee threw <u>me</u> the ball.
   The referee threw the ball to me.
5. The artist is drawing a sketch for <u>her patron</u>.
   The artist is drawing her patron a sketch.

## Test yourself 40.4

1. He will send the poem to his fiancée.
   <u>He will send his fiancée</u> the poem.
2. The professor is e-mailing the students his comments.
   <u>The professor is e-mailing his comments to the students</u>.
3. That company built a ship for the navy.
   <u>The company</u> built the navy a ship.
4. She drew a picture for her son.
   <u>She drew her son a picture</u>.
5. Amanda's friend was throwing a party for her.
   <u>Amanda's friend was throwing her a party</u>.

## Test yourself 40.5

1. We found a dress for <u>her</u>.
2. Mr. Duquesne has brought <u>him</u> the plans.
3. The old hunter told <u>us</u> the story.
4. The instructor is ordering this book for <u>the students in his class</u>.
5. I never promised <u>you</u> a rose garden.

## Test yourself 40.6

1. The children gave <u>the teacher</u> an apple.
2. I brought <u>this</u> for <u>you</u>.
3. The two men clasped <u>hands</u>.
4. This treaty will benefit <u>all mankind</u>.
5. She is telling <u>the reporter</u> the truth.

## Test yourself 41.1

|   | Subject pronoun | Object pronoun |
|---|---|---|
| 1. <u>She</u> laughed at the movie. | ✗ | |
| 2. Don't bother <u>me</u> now. | | ✗ |
| 3. <u>I</u> don't feel guilty. | ✗ | |
| 4. He has asked <u>her</u> to dance. | | ✗ |
| 5. Chris had been living near <u>you</u>. | | ✗ |

# UNIT 13: SUBJECTS AND OBJECTS

## Test yourself 41.2

1. My dear friend sent me a postcard from Italy.      indirect object
2. A teenager sat next to me in the theater.     object of a preposition
3. Irma has bought you the cookware.     indirect object
4. The dog approached them.     direct object
5. That family is always blaming us for their problems.     direct object

## Test yourself 42.1

*Subject*

1. These illnesses are treatable.     these illnesses
2. The judge had made a terrible mistake.     the judge
3. Be supportive.     you
4. Joan's father is an architect     Joan's father
5. Stand up for your rights.     you

## Test yourself 42.2

| | *Subject* | *Direct object* | *Indirect object* |
|---|---|---|---|
| 1. You can see marks in the dirt. | you | marks | |
| 2. That film sounds interesting. | that film | | |
| 3. The congregants built the temple. | the congregants | the temple | |
| 4. Give it to me! | you | it | me |
| 5. We need this computer. | we | this computer | |

☞ **FOR A REVIEW EXERCISE OF THIS UNIT, SEE THE WEBSITE.**

## UNIT 14: COMPOUND PHRASES

Coordinating conjunctions, such as *and*, *or*, and *but*, are very powerful. As we discussed in Lesson 18, they can join any two units of the same type. Here are some examples with *and*, the most common coordinating conjunction:
1. He gave tennis lessons to the girl **and** her brother. (two noun phrases joined)
2. I cooked dinner **and** washed the laundry. (two verb phrases joined)
3. Their beautiful **and** charming hostess soon put them at ease. (two adjectives joined)
4. My mother listened to me seriously **and** patiently. (two adverbs joined)
5. The monkey ran up the tree **and** around its trunk. (two prepositional phrases joined)
6. I rode my bike **and** Teresa walked. (two sentences joined)

In this unit, we'll take a closer look at joined noun phrases and joined verb phrases.

# Lesson 43: Compound noun phrases

What do you notice about this next sentence?
  1. My friend worked at the diner and his cousin worked at the diner.

While it's a perfectly grammatical sentence, we often choose to make it less repetitious and say instead:
  2. My friend and his cousin worked at the diner.

Since *and*, a coordinating conjunction, is joining two noun phrases here, *my friend and his cousin* is called a compound noun phrase.

> **Quick tip 43.1**
>
> Two noun phrases joined by a coordinating conjunction is called a compound noun phrase.

Here are some more examples, with the compound noun phrases underlined.
  3. She slipped the photograph and both letters into her pocket.
  4. The senator or his assistant will attend the event.
  5. I'll be traveling to Kansas and Missouri next week on business.

## Test yourself 43.1

Underline the compound noun phrases in each of the sentences below.
Sample: The public discovered that the company and its subsidiaries were cheating customers.

*Getting started* (answers on p. 197)

1. They had walked for miles and miles.
2. Henry felt guilt and shame for what he had done.
3. Vermont has lots of old houses and rustic barns.
4. The young bride is going shopping with her mother or mother-in-law.
5. Paying for gas and electricity costs a lot more this year than last.

*More practice* (answers on the website)

6. Michael and I have been best friends for years.
7. Delta Airlines and Air France have flights to Paris from the U.S.
8. The lead actress or director will likely win Oscars.
9. Audi and BMW are owned by German companies.
10. The president and his foreign visitor held a joint press conference.

# Lesson 44: Compound verb phrases

What do you notice about this next sentence?
    1. Frank ran to the store and Frank purchased a few items.
While it's a perfectly grammatical sentence, we often choose to make it less repetitious and say instead:
    2. Frank ran to the store and purchased a few items.
Since *and*, a coordinating conjunction, is joining two verb phrases here, *ran to the store and purchased a few items* is called a compound verb phrase.

> **Quick tip 44.1**
>
> Two verb phrases joined by a coordinating conjunction is called a compound verb phrase.

Here are some more examples, with the compound verb phrases underlined.
    3. The general <u>ran forward and led the troops</u>.
    4. She <u>remained calm and followed her instincts</u>.
    5. His advisor <u>presents him with good ideas but rarely helps him carry them out</u>.

## Test yourself 44.1

Underline the compound verb phrases in each of the sentences below.
Sample: I'll <u>phone them and listen to their ideas</u>.

***Getting started*** (answers on p. 197)

1. They often call each other and talk all afternoon.
2. Adam wrote letters to the company and spoke to their representatives.
3. He invented the product but lost money in the process.
4. Stephen flew to Europe and visited his childhood friend.
5. I received your message yesterday but couldn't respond to it immediately.

***More practice*** (answers on the website)

6. On Saturday nights Samantha dresses up and meets with her friends.
7. Once a month or so we stay home and order dinner in.
8. Politicians do not always walk the walk and talk the talk.
9. On hot summer days, the O'Briens drive to the beach and enjoy the sun.
10. This couple fights but always makes up.

## Test yourself 44.2

Underline the compound noun phrases and verb phrases in the sentences below. A sentence may contain more than one compound phrase.
Sample: <u>He and she</u> will probably <u>leave on Friday and return on Sunday</u>.

## UNIT 14: COMPOUND PHRASES

***Getting started*** (answers on p. 197)

1. The horse stepped back and rolled its eyes.
2. Amanda is wearing long sleeves but carrying a parasol.
3. When Kathy and her daughter travel to Boston, they always visit Harvard and MIT.
4. On Sundays Mr. Adams and his neighbor play golf and have lunch in the clubhouse.
5. He loves to cook and entertain.

***More practice*** (answers on the website)

6. His youngest son is afraid of thunder and lightning.
7. Your husband should work hard at his job or find another one.
8. Harry and his friend often travel to Washington and visit the Smithsonian.
9. It is common knowledge that the Yankees and the Red Sox are bitter rivals.
10. That would ruin her reputation and end her career.

# Answer keys: *Test yourself, Getting started* questions – Unit 14

### Test yourself 43.1

1. They had walked for miles and miles.
2. Henry felt guilt and shame for what he had done.
3. Vermont has lots of old houses and rustic barns.
4. The young bride is going shopping with her mother or mother-in-law.
5. Paying for gas and electricity costs a lot more this year than last.

### Test yourself 44.1

1. They often call each other and talk all afternoon.
2. Adam wrote letters to the company and spoke to their representatives.
3. He invented the product but lost money in the process.
4. Stephen flew to Europe and visited his childhood friend.
5. I received your message yesterday but couldn't respond to it immediately.

### Test yourself 44.2

1. The horse stepped back and rolled its eyes.
2. Amanda is wearing long sleeves but carrying a parasol.
3. When Kathy and her daughter travel to Boston, they always visit Harvard and MIT.
4. On Sundays Mr. Adams and his neighbor play golf and have lunch in the clubhouse.
5. He loves to cook and entertain.

☞ **FOR A REVIEW EXERCISE OF THIS UNIT, SEE THE WEBSITE.**

# Review matching exercise and answer key – Part II

**Review matching exercise**

Match the underlined word or words in each sentence to the appropriate term in each set. Use each term only once.
Sample: Warren <u>gave himself an extra serving</u>.                         verb phrase

## Set A

| compound noun phrase | object pronoun | prepositional phrase |
| indirect object | perfect tense | future tense |
| modal | predicate adjective | |

1. He <u>has written</u> to you every day.
2. Mrs. McLean is sending the recipe to <u>her sister-in-law</u>.
3. He understands <u>me</u> better than anyone.
4. His companions <u>will take</u> their canoe across the river.
5. Richard was working when <u>Miguel and Sam</u> came by.
6. The building is <u>near the stream</u>.
7. It <u>might</u> be the largest museum in the world.
8. Those decisions can be <u>difficult</u>.

## Set B

| compound verb phrase | past participle | subject pronoun |
| direct object | present participle | |
| main verb | progressive tense | |

1. I'll <u>buy the food and then cook it</u>.
2. <u>They</u> had come back to buy two copies of the newspaper.
3. Matt <u>is hurrying</u> to his office.
4. The old man was chanting <u>a song</u> she'd never heard before.
5. Molly <u>selected</u> her dress early in the day.
6. Her horse <u>was behaving</u> calmly.
7. Johnny had <u>eaten</u> a good breakfast.

## Answer key: Review matching exercise – Part II

### Set A

1. He <u>has written</u> to you every day.  perfect tense
2. Mrs. McLean is sending the recipe to <u>her sister-in-law</u>.  indirect object
3. He understands <u>me</u> better than anyone.  object pronoun
4. His companions <u>will take</u> their canoe across the river.  future tense
5. Richard was working when <u>Miguel and Sam</u> came by.  compound noun phrase
6. The building is <u>near the stream</u>.  prepositional phrase
7. It <u>might</u> be the largest museum in the world.  modal
8. Those decisions can be <u>difficult</u>.  predicate adjective

### Set B

1. I'll <u>buy the food and then cook</u> it.  compound verb phrase
2. <u>They</u> had come back to buy two copies of the newspaper.  subject pronoun
3. Matt is <u>hurrying</u> to his office.  present participle
4. The old man was chanting <u>a song</u> she'd never heard before.  direct object
5. Molly <u>selected</u> her dress early in the day.  main verb
6. Her horse <u>was behaving</u> calmly.  progressive tense
7. Johnny had <u>eaten</u> a good breakfast.  past participle

www.ingramcontent.com/pod-product-compliance
Lightning Source LLC
Chambersburg PA
CBHW071437080526
44587CB00014B/1885